"I would not hesitate to recommend Simon and The Simple Way if you want to take your personal performance to the next level."

— **Adrian Hick, Head of Sales & Relationships,**
Lloyds TSB International

"Over the years I have been working with Simon, his insights, rules of thumb and often interesting and quirky exercises have helped immensely! Tools to help me put my thoughts in order and challenges in perspective, and to think through how my actions will affect the business. Most of all Simon has helped me identify and be true to what really matters, and through this book, many others will have access to some of that help."

— **Terry Watts, Chief Executive, Proskills**

"Where there is a challenge Simon is able to get to the heart of it quick, slicing away distraction and noise. His ability to do so reminds me of a samurai warrior. Clean, quick and simple."

— **Kim Ann Curtin, Founder & CEO,**
The Wall Street Coach

"Simon cuts to the chase and our conversations have left me with greater belief in my thinking, my methods and my management style. His methodologies present simple solutions for complicated people. His Simple Notes are thought-provoking, sometimes challenging, often off-the-wall and always a pleasure to read and digest."

— **Ted Rodger, Managing Director, FPP**

"Simon's approach keeps you moving forward, removes hurdles (including the perceived ones) and holds you true to yourself. In short he 'keeps everything simple' and success follows."

Coutts Bank

Ambi,

#22 - start here
& walk slowly!

Simon T.
Park Plaza, London
19 October 2012

THE
SIMPLE
WAY

**52 IDEAS
TO FIND YOUR WAY
THROUGH OUR
COMPLEX WORLD**

SIMON TYLER

Marshall Cavendish
Business

Published in 2012 by Marshall Cavendish Business
An imprint of Marshall Cavendish International

1 New Industrial Road, Singapore 536196
genrefsales@marshallcavendish.com
www.marshallcavendish.com/genref

Other Marshall Cavendish offices:
Marshall Cavendish Corporation, 99 White Plains Road, Tarrytown, NY 10591
• Marshall Cavendish International (Thailand) Co Ltd. 253 Asoke, 12th Flr,
Sukhumvit 21 Road, Klongtoey Nua, Wattana, Bangkok 10110, Thailand •
Marshall Cavendish (Malaysia) Sdn Bhd, Times Subang, Lot 46, Subang Hi-Tech
Industrial Park, Batu Tiga, 40000 Shah Alam, Selangor Darul Ehsan, Malaysia

Marshall Cavendish is a trademark of Times Publishing Limited

A CIP record for this book is available from the British Library

ISBN 978 981 4382 17 5

Printed and bound in Great Britain by
TJI International Limited, Padstow, Cornwall

This book is dedicated to all the people who have inspired me, chosen to work with me and who are yet to work with me. Especially Sally my wife, and my children Rebecca, Alex and Xavier, who are a constant source of love, energy and ideas in everything I do.

CONTENTS

ACKNOWLEDGEMENTS

Most of the ideas within this book originated in the ether of my mind. Where they did not, I have made reference to the source of the note and I acknowledge those sources here. All notes have been checked by Sally. Jason Bootle has waited tirelessly for me to produce a new note every two weeks for the blog since early 2009.

Others I would like to thank for their help, inspiration, ideas, support and challenges include Drew Rozell, Michael Neill, Mike Dooley, the late Thomas Leonard, Joanne Dunleavy, Kate Duffy, Debbie Pye, Ken Buist, Mark Harris and Seán Weafer. Further information on some of these sources and others referenced here can be found at the back of this book.

Final thanks of course go to Penny St Lawrence for her grammatical excellence and to Clare Christian who has shepherded me through the publishing process.

INTRODUCTION:
CHOOSING THE SIMPLE WAY

I live my life The Simple Way. It represents the choices I make as I tackle the complexities of my world. It is effective and simple and it is something you too can do.

My experiences inside and outside of work have led to the development of The Simple Way. I've been an employee in big corporations, in small self-start entrepreneurial businesses, within my own companies and have also sat on the board of directors of others. As a coach, consultant and facilitator I have been in some amazing learning situations. Add to these my life roles of father, husband, brother, son and uncle, and the accumulated lessons and observations have been plentiful and provide a richly stocked library of case studies.

Over the years I have observed life and business scenarios that are extraordinarily complex, complications that have festered and grown and led to delays, confusion, disappointment and even commercial paralysis.

But to simplify is to change.

My role as a coach has always been to assist, accelerate and guide clients to the success they desire. The methods, techniques and challenges I have employed are intended to support the client journey, and this book collects and presents these methods as a series of Simple Notes so that you too can benefit.

In 2009 I started keeping a blog and every two weeks since then I have posted whatever was in my thoughts. It could be a conversation I just had with a client, a challenge I faced at that time, or something I had just read, heard or experienced. And very occasionally it could be something from the proverbial left field, something inexplicable – and these have often been the blogs that received the most feedback and seemingly had the greatest impact for my readers.

I suggest that rather than read this book in a linear fashion, you dip in and select the thoughts and ideas that are relevant for you on any given day. To help make more sense of the collection, I have created 11 common business and personal evolution challenges that people face and against each I have listed the articles that offer ways to face the challenge anew.

Throughout the book I pose questions that you may be tempted to consider only briefly and answer superficially. For full effect I urge you to stop and think through your response to the question. Perhaps even pick up a pen and get the thoughts down on paper.

Once you have consumed a few of the notes, you will begin to notice some foundational themes regarding positive personal change. My core coaching beliefs and my Simple Notes tend to be based on the following:

- You get what you think about, whether you want it or not.
- Thoughts trigger feelings and feelings trigger actions, which in turn create the results in your world.
- When you understand where your thoughts come from and what triggers them, you are a long way down the evolution road.

And regarding simplicity:

- When life is tough, simplifying makes things better.
- When life is great, simplifying makes things better.

My hope is that you keep this book with you or close to hand and go to it as you need, whether it be for a recharge or an idea or a way through, or perhaps even a topic to share with your team (feel free to do so, all I ask is that you let them know where the idea came from, and that they can subscribe to my site for more).

I am confident that within these pages you will find many ideas that will resonate and surprise you with what is possible. As you begin to experience success and positive change please do let me know; your feedback will inspire others.

The Simple Way is your choice, one that you can make whenever you want or need.

SIMON TYLER

Spring 2012

www.simontyler.com

HOW TO USE THIS HANDBOOK

This book is designed to be short and easily digestible and you will soon find your own way of working through the Notes. There is a Simple Note for every week of the year so you may prefer to read it in weekly instalments: reading and acting on one a week will provide personal growth for you. But like many books and texts in the personal development world some will resonate with you and you may scowl at others! Let go of any resistance and follow the flow; act on those you like and skip the rest.

Your options in consuming this book are:
- Read it linearly and follow one Simple Note challenge each week.
- Read it linearly and mark the pages that resonate with you, then act on them when you are ready.

- Use the Simple Way Matrix that follows and begin your week by choosing an evolution focus or change goal and the Simple Note that supports it.
- Randomly open the book and work with the Simple Note from that page.
- Use it as a reference book. Turn to the Simple Note that matches the development need of a colleague, a client or your team. Share it with them and work through it together.

Whatever you choose, enjoy the Simple Notes, be challenged and driven to action. But always, remember to keep it simple.

SELECTING THE SIMPLE NOTE FOR YOUR SITUATION

In most cases the title of the Simple Note suggests the situation to which it applies, but not always. The Simple Way Matrix that follows lists 11 common problems and challenges. Find the area that matches your circumstance and pick one or more of the Simple Notes that refer to the challenge.

		Page	Over-whelmed	Lack of Belief (Doubt!)	Confusion (Mind is Full)	Disorganised	Lacking Focus
1	Are You At Your Best?	20					
2	Noise	23	✦	✦	✦	✦	
3	Slump	26	✦	✦			
4	Set-up	29				✦	
5	Words	32		✦	✦		✦
6	Word up	34	✦				
7	When?	37					✦
8	Loose Ends	40	✦			✦	
9	Conquering the Email Dragon	44	✦			✦	
10	Your Very Own CIA	48					
11	Sprint	51	✦				✦
12	Pause	54	✦		✦	✦	
13	Clear the Clutter	58			✦	✦	
14	Double-Tasking	61	✦			✦	
15	BlackBerry Moments	64	✦			✦	
16	Resetting Your Daily Default Mode	67					✦
17	Time and Space	70	✦			✦	
18	Moving On	74					✦
19	Boost Your Energy	78	✦			✦	
20	Simplify Your Overwhelm	81	✦			✦	
21	Three Simple Steps to Somewhere	84		✦			✦
22	Urgentia	87	✦			✦	
23	Six of One, Half a Dozen of the Other	92		✦			✦
24	Tolerations	95					
25	Instant Liberation	98	✦	✦	✦		
26	Bringing Goals to Life	100		✦			✦
27	Expectation Playlist	103	✦				
28	Retreat	105	✦	✦	✦	✦	
29	Become Frustration-Free	107	✦		✦	✦	
30	Boost Personal Productivity	110	✦			✦	✦

Unclear Goals or Direction	Lack of a Sense of Purpose	Uninspired, Drained & Lethargic	Not Getting Anywhere	Preoccupied, Distracted	Relationships Not As They Could Be
	✦		✦		✦
		✦	✦		
✦	✦				
			✦		
✦		✦			✦
	✦		✦	✦	
			✦		
		✦		✦	
			✦		
				✦	✦
		✦		✦	
			✦		
					✦
✦	✦	✦			
	✦			✦	
✦	✦				✦
		✦		✦	✦
		✦	✦		
✦	✦		✦		
			✦		✦
		✦			
✦		✦		✦	✦
		✦			
✦			✦		✦
		✦	✦		✦
✦	✦	✦		✦	✦
		✦		✦	✦
			✦		

Unclear Goals or Direction	Lack of a Sense of Purpose	Uninspired, Drained & Lethargic	Not Getting Anywhere	Preoccupied, Distracted	Relationships Not As They Could Be
✦		✦	✦		
		✦			✦
			✦		✦
				✦	
					✦
			✦	✦	
		✦	✦		
	✦	✦			✦
		✦	✦		✦
			✦		
✦					
			✦	✦	
		✦		✦	
	✦		✦		
		✦	✦		
			✦		✦
		✦		✦	
✦	✦	✦	✦		
		✦	✦	✦	✦
		✦		✦	✦
	✦			✦	✦
	✦	✦	✦		
	✦	✦	✦	✦	✦

1

ARE YOU AT YOUR BEST?

> "Twenty years from now you will be more disappointed by the things that you didn't do than by the ones you did do. So throw off the bowlines. Sail away from the safe harbour. Catch the trade winds in your sails. Explore. Dream. Discover."
>
> Mark Twain (1835–1910)

Are you currently at your best? Right now, today, this week? Are you in a purple patch, in your element, firing on all cylinders?

If not, when were you last at your best, and what's changed since then?

Having observed myself working and, more often, attempting to work, I've noticed a correlation between being at my best and the subsequent results (financial or otherwise), feeling good, efficiency and effectiveness. My ability to influence, to be creative and to inspire others is strongest when I am operating at my best. At all other times some or all of these outcomes elude me.

I've noticed this in almost all of the people with whom I have worked as a coach over the last 10 years. When they spend moments 'at their best' for a few hours, a day, perhaps even a week or more, amazing things happen. They experience breakthroughs or crystal-clear perspectives on topics that were once hazy, and notice performance increases in themselves and those around them.

So why would we not want to be at our best all the time?

Well, you can be at your best significantly more often than you might be now. Firstly, it is a choice, a conscious and determined choice. You control your life and performance, no one else, and you are not the victim of the situations in which you find yourself. Secondly, it's about becoming aware of who you are when you are at your best, what are the circumstances, what has led up to this and so on, in as much detail as you can identify. Finally, it is about creating that context every day so you can be at your best.

Here's a suggestion, coined by my masterful coaching friend Kate Duffy. Pick up your pen and write uninterrupted for at least three minutes, completing the following sentence:

"I'm at my best when…"

Revisit this often and keep track of what the ingredients are. If you try to make these happen one at a time, you will move to a place when you are at your best more often and your best will just get better!

2

NOISE

> "Always bear in mind that your own resolution to succeed is more important than any other one thing."
>
> Abraham Lincoln (1809–1865)

There is so much noise around us. Traffic, conversations, music, the buzz of a PC or other office machinery, even the overhead lights. What about the most challenging noises of all – that inner voice, the half-thoughts, the emotional blurt-outs and second thoughts? What a cacophony of sound!

The ability to concentrate on more than one conscious thought is more of a challenge today than ever before. I have noticed attention spans (the purest, most alert, creative and aware type of attention) in professional business people being reduced to just a few minutes as they drift in and out of clarity. It may seem like you stay on-task for the hour or two you set aside but in truth, this is not the case. Distractions knock your focus often. Your way of working simply isn't working!

Yes, business life is fast-paced – decisions need to be made, information assimilated, messages delivered, people influenced. Today's leaders often feel the strain as a decision is not quite right, information is missed, messages are poorly thought through and influence is diminished.

It is time to work on this and reactivate the skills and creativity that reside in the quieter parts of your mind.

There are many techniques I have found, been taught and experimented with and, as I discover more, they will be updated on my blog. Your thinking needs more space: space to allow new thoughts and ideas to form, and space to listen, watch and notice what's going on around you. And we aren't necessarily talking about setting aside hours here; you can start this process of change with just a few moments every day. Here are a few starters:

Write – in Julia Cameron's book *The Artist's Way*, she suggests starting each day by writing three pages (just write, don't judge it, don't even read it, just write).

Pause – count to two (to yourself, not out loud) before

answering, or contributing a comment. This is sufficient time for your brain to consider your comment and shift away from a 'reaction' to a more considered 'response'.

Breathe – twice a day, take a moment to breathe in, hold and breathe out, slowly. Repeat 10 times and notice how your state will change away from being anxious, tense, angry, stressed or concerned, to being calmer, clearer and more open.

Talk – dialogue with a coach or colleague is a great way to create a quiet space in a noisy day.

3

INTERRUPT YOUR SLUMP

> "One of the secrets of success is to refuse to let temporary setbacks defeat us."
>
> Mary Kay (1915–2001)

We are all emotionally connected, to some degree, to the people and events around us. These outside events often trigger what seems to be an automated emotional reaction, and from there our thoughts, feelings and moods blossom. Are these always empowering and useful though? Probably not.

Chances are, you may actually be reducing your power of response, restricting your creative subconscious and adopting a weakened state. Your ability to respond appropriately, to decide, to think in straight lines or to engage your full intuitive self can be restricted.

In the midst of the reaction process is a physical shift that triggers your emotional reaction. It could be a shrug, a frown or even some kind of slump. There are many varieties of 'slump reactions': shoulders drooping, head shifting down and chin forward, an exhale with a dropped curved back and many more subtle actions, but all of them notably slump-worthy.

It's likely that you have unknowingly refined and engrained your slump reaction over the years, and with it comes a pre-arranged set of thoughts, feelings and moods that your brain has linked to the slump. No matter how subtle or even undetectable it is, your slump reaction is setting you up to be 'less than your best'.

During a 2009 Test Match I noticed the England cricket team slump when their match-winning batting star was out early. Unsurprisingly (to me), the subsequent batsmen struggled to get their heads back into the game. This is just as applicable in the business world.

At a business meeting, I noticed slump reactions to a particular corporate message regarding cost-cutting and potential reorganisation. The subsequent conversations on a separate topic were less creative or positively solution-oriented than they could have been.

I challenge you for the next couple of weeks to discover your slump reaction and notice when it happens. Laugh when you catch it happening, interrupt it and choose an alternative. Try a more powerful upright stance and take in a deep breath. Your brain may initially still throw up some reactions to the situation, but you will see it more clearly for what it is and actually have a choice.

After a week of interruptions you will start to notice a change in your moods and capabilities in situations that previously would have annoyed, frustrated, flummoxed or even floored you.

4

SET-UP

> "The greater thing in this world is not so much where we stand as in what direction we are going."
>
> Oliver Wendell Holmes (1809–1894)

How are you set up? For success, for failure or simply for whatever shows up? Are you set up for a good time or not? By this I am not referring to how you are innately wired, but more to how you 'set yourself up' to perform.

What is your set-up? Are you even aware of it? Do outside forces affect your set-up day to day? And if they do, is that all the time or a result of random external circumstances?

In my coaching I have noticed that a person's set-up very accurately and literally sets up their experience and results every day. If you tell yourself today is going to be frantic, stressful or a struggle, it probably will be.

Let's take the frantic set-up. Your brain responds to the set-up brilliantly. It focuses your attention exclusively on any evidence of 'frantic'. It seeks it out, defocuses everything else and emphasises the proof. It holds your muscles and body in a permanently tensed fashion, ready to 'franticise'.

In this state it becomes difficult to think your way out of being frantic, to problem-solve, to be serene and sometimes even to calm down at all. The probability is that even if the situations you find yourself in aren't frantic, somehow you'll make them so or magnetically find something or someone to exercise your adrenaline-charged frantic set-up.

This is the same for all your set-ups, whether you are aware of them or not. Whatever your set-up, you will attract situations, people and incidences that match your setting – what power you have!

I challenge you to notice and become aware of your set-ups. There are often times in the day when you shift a set-up and can therefore upgrade it, if you exercise awareness and your freedom to choose. The common set-up moments are first thing in the morning, break times, formal meetings and work-to-home transition times.

Step into your set-up process and choose your own setting. While external factors can affect your day, it is your set-up that gives them the impact they need. When you deliberately select your set-up you become resistant to slipping into old habits and soon bring supportive events, people and situations to your chosen setting.

5

....

WORDS

> "Be not careless in deeds, nor confused in words, nor rambling in thought."
>
> Marcus Aurelius (121–180)

I once heard the expression that language for humans is both the greatest gift and the greatest curse. In my work, I have experienced both sides of this.

The words you choose (sometimes unconsciously, out of habit) reflect your current thinking, but also significantly affect your future thinking, not to mention others who are in earshot.

Brain science has proved that in a predictable way, your thoughts impact how you feel, which directly impacts the actions you take and the results you get, or indeed the next situation you find yourself in.

Once those thoughts are voiced out loud the impact is doubled. But most importantly, the person most influenced by your words is YOU!

What are you saying?

How do you describe things?

I recently described a situation as tense, overwhelming, snowed-under, messy and disorganised. Before I knew it my thinking matched this perfectly and I didn't feel good, and crucially I couldn't 'think' my way out of it.

I shifted my words, not being delusional or false in my upgraded descriptions, but just ensuring they were better chosen. I reminded myself of my abilities to work through situations and of the resources I always seem to find. And slowly my thought patterns altered. Feelings of being overwhelmed disappeared, allowing me to further upgrade the words I used, and I then went about solving the problem.

Notice your words. Do they describe the situation you want to stay in, or are they leading you further into a situation you want to avoid? You get to choose, and don't forget who's listening.

6

WORD-UP

> "Have something to say, and say it as clearly
> as you can. That is the only secret of style."
>
> Matthew Arnold (1822–1888)

When I blogged the earlier 'Words' post in 2009 I received many comments. Readers stated that they worked on their words, but caught themselves drifting back to their old language soon after – they wanted some more permanent fixes.

In response, I created a follow-up inspired by Super Coach Michael Neill. It details some simple experiments to upgrade your words. Choose one to try out and start today, or work through them all if you're up for it and ready to word-up. They WILL have an impact on your brain's word production.

Today – for the next 24 hours, do not complain to anyone. About anything. If you catch yourself complaining before the 24 hours are up, simply start the timer again. When I first took this on as a challenge it took me nine days to complete it. Since then, however, I have almost eliminated my propensity to complain and now take responsibility for everything in which I am involved. Each time I retake this challenge, I get closer to a straight complain-free 24-hours.

This Week – for the next week, do not gossip or entertain gossip about anyone, from anyone. If someone persists in attempting to gossip with you, you may ask them to stop, explain this experiment or simply walk away. If you catch yourself gossiping before the week is up, simply start again. Talking about people has been reported as the lowest grade of energy in a dialogue, and often leaves both talkers drained in some way, which is further evidence of the need to word-up.

This Month – for the next month, do not criticise any member of your family, inner circle of friends or your team. You may of course make requests of them if there is something that you would like them to do differently. Be honest with yourself as to whether or not your request was a genuine request or a secret criticism. If you catch yourself criticising a team member, close friend or family member before the end of the month, simply begin again.

Each of these experiments targets the root of your thinking and capacity for word production, and can support a permanent change in both.

7

WHEN?

> "Yesterday is gone. Tomorrow has not yet come. We have only today. Let us begin."
>
> **Mother Teresa (1910–1997)**

In her coaching business, Kate Duffy constantly uses the phrase 'If not now, when?'. What a great challenge!

Are you putting up with stuff and waiting for an undefined perfect moment or set of circumstances, resources or ideas to solve or change it? Do you have intentions that you haven't progressed because they are not urgent, that sit in the background waiting until the 'ideal' time?

Doing this in any area of your work or life is holding you back in some way – your happiness, enjoyment, your full throttle effort, until… when? In short, have you suspended the full you until your 'when' happens?

'When' is a cute little word. It can trick you into putting up with your current situation, on the basis that it will (at some point, in a non-defined future) be solved. It goes into your mental pending tray, ready to remind and irritate you every day, occupying space and never shifting. It becomes an invisible excuse preventing you from taking inspired action toward your goals, whatever they may be.

Kate's challenge, 'If not now, when?', can be levelled at all of the areas in which you are stalling. It doesn't necessarily mean you have to take action on all of them this very moment. It simply means you need to examine the blockage and check whether it is important enough to take action against now. Or even if it needs to be there at all – you might give yourself permission to simply let it go. If it's not ready for release or new action, then diminish its importance and allow it to be parked, and don't mention it again till the next review.

From time to time I catch myself putting up with situations, and I can palpably feel gloom clouds gathering around me. Most of the time I am aware of this and take action early to shift my thinking. The process I use is to ask myself a series of questions that help me think through my position. If you try it make sure that you don't just think the answers; write them down or get someone to ask you the questions so you can answer them out loud. This is what I ask myself:

- What doesn't feel good, or right?
- What am I putting up with, or what is it that seems to be dragging, difficult or problematic right now?
- What am I waiting for? (This must be a real examination of factors or circumstances that need to be true in order to take positive action.)
- Even if the above factors are true, what steps can I take today to change my direction?
- What would it feel like to know that 'when' has become 'now'?

Good luck and go ahead and make your change. If not now, when?

8

LOOSE ENDS

> "Finish each day and be done with it. You have done what you could. Some blunders and absurdities no doubt crept in; forget them as soon as you can. Tomorrow is a new day; begin it well and serenely and with too high a spirit to be cumbered with your old nonsense."
>
> Ralph Waldo Emerson (1803–1882)

I have learnt repeatedly (perhaps I am either a slow or reluctant learner of this particular lesson) that I tend to mentally work on or process outstanding work and personal life matters throughout the day. The more there is, the more energy it takes up and often the less powerful and resourceful

I am, and subsequently, the more drained I feel.

Every piece of paper, unopened email and unfinished task or conversation is using up your human RAM or data storage. When these incomplete processes accumulate you tend not to notice until they become obvious. When you reach your own 'full' point, many things change.

Your state of mind alters and you are more likely to react to the day's events rashly, disproportionately, become irritable or just feel overwhelmed most of the time. If you don't catch this state change in time, you become physically tired, and the emotional changes can make you feel like anything you do makes little difference to your virtual to-do list – that you are simply not getting anywhere.

When you take action to complete a task, you regain a more powerful state, are able to gain mental clarity over what's going on and experience overview rather than overwhelm. The action you take isn't necessarily doing all the tasks or ticking off every single item on your list; it's about shifting your attitude and taking inspired action instead of frantic scattergun action.

My technique for you to consider is rather like clicking 'Control–Alt–Delete' on a PC to see what processes are running in the background. There are often unnecessary programmes running that you can instantly close, and a few that you can switch off in one step. The same applies to all the things running through your mind. Look at them, review your thoughts and shift your attitude towards them. This reboot can move you to a significantly more resourceful place – and from there you can begin again.

I recommend that you undertake a major personal reboot from time to time, at least once a year. The following is my quick five-stage reboot or 'Control–Alt–Delete' process:

Thought Unload – Sit silently for a few minutes and allow the spray of thoughts to pour out onto paper. Write down everything you think may be in there. You may or may not take action on some of them; just unloading them can be liberating.

Work Area Cleanse – Desks get cluttered – with urgent, non-urgent, important, unimportant stuff. Be ruthless and march through the paperwork inbox, making instant decisions about every item: bin it, file it, do it tomorrow or do it this week (no more deliberating!).

Email Purge – In busy phases emails tend to build up and many require decisions, commitments, comment or some kind of response. Spend some more ruthless time cleaning up this volume. Work quickly; in doing so you are activating your intuitive decision-making unit.

Waiting for Me – Who is waiting for you, expecting something from you or owed something by you? Over the next seven days complete your outstanding tasks with these people. This includes delivering words of thanks, appreciation and gratitude – some of these may go back a while and they really are liberating once completed.

Waiting for You – Who are you waiting for, who owes you, from whom are you wishing or wanting a word of thanks or gratitude? In truth you cannot control their completion, but you can instantly shift your attitude to the incompletes and cease the draining effect of each. Let go of the expectations and clear them out. If any come in, that's a bonus.

Enjoy stepping up into your new powerful and resourceful state each time you reboot.

9

CONQUERING THE EMAIL DRAGON

> "Man must cease attributing his problems to his environment, and learn again to exercise his will and his personal responsibility."
>
> Albert Schweitzer (1875–1965)

Email forms an unavoidable part of our work and private lives. It is often the most prolific form of our communication. But your relationship to your email inbox can make the difference between your work rates, your stress levels and your overall communication efficiency.

Here are some suggestions that have worked for me and for the people I have coached. I don't necessarily recommend them, only that you consider them. Your world may have codes of conduct that mean some of these can be too hasty, reckless or simply inappropriate. Just consider the suggestions that are suitable for you.

These 10 are above the obvious few and don't include steps such as switch off auto-notifiers, asking people you know to reduce email, use a junk mail filter, shortening your email content, etc.

1. Stop using 'Reply All'. Be ready to apologise to those who feel left out of some email loops – explain why you're doing it.

2. Be more specific in the subject line. Even if recipients never get to open your email or even delete it on sight, they will always view the subject line. Be clearer and tell them what you want to do with the content. Consider including the acronym 'EOM' in the title bar to inform the reader that the title bar is in fact the End of Message!

3. Deal with mail as it arrives. Respond to it, act on it, read it, whatever. If you haven't dealt with it in seven days, delete it.

4. Only process email at set times. A high volume of email has an incredible gnawing power to grab your attention. Where you place your attention is your immense potential power, so don't give it away lightly.

5. Find out about software that filters mail – there will be several types in your company, in your network or available on the web to test and incorporate.

6. Clear your inbox every day – action them, file them, put them in the seven-day waiting folder or delete them.

7. Set up different email addresses – keep private email separate from work and perhaps set up more than one work address: e.g. one for customers, one for your team and one for everything else.

8. Send fewer emails – think about what you want to cause, provoke, change, influence. Is email the best option?

9. Don't reply to every message (with 'thanks' or 'will do') – people are aware of their colleagues' email volume and rarely expect, or even want, the politeness of such a response.

10. Unsubscribe from lists that you have not read for more than 3 months. Stop accumulating unopened mail; you're storing them somewhere in your head. They've served their time and will come back into focus again when you need them.

And if the dragon is still roaring:

11. Delete All – extreme action in extreme cases; evaluate the risk and do it. The important stuff comes around again.

Don't forget to let those in your team and extended network know what you are doing and don't be surprised if your email dragon-slaying strategy seems odd to them.

Social media (Twitter, Facebook, LinkedIn, Flickr etc.) is transforming the way we communicate. Email will gradually move down the communication preference list and join letters and paper memos as the 'old way' in which we communicated. So even if you do nothing with your current Email Dragon, its flames will soon no longer burn so brightly.

10

....

YOUR VERY OWN CIA

> "If you want the rainbow, you've got to put up with the rain."
>
> Jimmy Durante (1893–1980)

Do you change your attitude and maybe even your behaviour when things just aren't going to plan? How about when decisions are made that directly affect you and limit your immediate choices? Or when a set of unexpected and annoying circumstances show up?

In these moments a whole set of responses fire off that alter the way you act for the next few minutes, hours, or if it's really bad, days. And, unsurprisingly, once you get into that unwanted state you seem to attract more of it!

Clearly, this is not taking you to your best, most productive and most powerful state. Instead, it is sapping any enjoyment you could have. It's just not a good place to be.

It sounds easy when some random coach like me pipes up and says, 'you have a choice here'. But you really do, and here's a thinking process to help.

For a long time I have worked with my clients on 'acceptance', which is the opposite of 'resistance'. The latter causes friction and unease; the former is a free-flowing state in which you maintain access to your full thinking and action-taking capability.

A friend of mine, the 'R-Evolutionary' coach Seán Weafer, coined a great acronym to help in such situations – 'CIA'. CIA is a question process to take you out of moaning, resisting and gritting teeth to a more powerful non-resisting place of acceptance.

Control – can I control this situation? If I can, in any way, then let's take action and do it – if not, move on…

Influence – can I influence anything around this situation? Can I speak to anyone, send information or change its impact in some way? If I can, in any way, then let's get into action and do it – if not, move on…

Accept it, for now – this doesn't mean give in, it is an in-the-moment invitation to accept whatever it is. From here I can choose to get on with something else, relax into the aftermath, see it for what it is and so on.

I implement my CIA often, as soon as I begin to feel ratty about a situation or meeting or interaction. I regularly experience a significant reduction in the amount of time I feel physically tense, which people tell me is a healthier way to be, and certainly uses less energy and prevents me from becoming drained and no fun to be with.

Good luck with calling in your CIA this week. Run through the questions often. It can help working this through with a colleague – have them ask the questions and hold you to your answers. Regain your power and avoid letting situations turn you into a grouch!

11

SPRINT

> "After one has discovered what he is called for, he should set out to do it with all of the power that he has in his system."
>
> Martin Luther King, Jr. (1929–1968)

I often notice people circling around ever-growing to-do lists. This circling can lead to an unwanted feeling of being out of step, falling behind and missing out on the important actions at the cost of the urgent.

This inadvertent delaying tactic can be linked to some bigger, unspoken – and therefore unanswered – questions about purpose, direction and meaning to all these itty-bitty tasks. In order to get to that, a crucial first step is to recreate some momentum.

Some time ago Michael Neill (www.geniuscatalyst. com) inspired me with a Julius Caesar story. Putting aside some of his methods and political ambitions, it is difficult not to be amazed at the amount Caesar achieved. During his lifetime he was renowned for his *celeritas*, a Latin word meaning 'speed' or 'quickness'. Time and time again he would act so quickly that his opponents were caught completely unawares.

The flip side of this was that he would sometimes act impulsively or rashly and get himself into difficulties as a result. But no one was better than he himself at getting out of these difficulties – again with speed and effectiveness.

You can use this principle of *celeritas* in your own life.

To do so, simply practise working and moving a little bit faster than you usually do.

This is remarkably effective because if you move faster than normal, you don't give yourself time to procrastinate. If you are moving fast, you don't think 'I'll do that later' or 'I really don't want to do that'. You just do it.

Try it for a short period to start with. Thirty minutes seems to be my optimum *celeritas* time. Set a timer and just go all out to do as much work that you can within that time. Don't spend any time thinking what to do next, just get on with whatever comes to hand. Sending (or deleting) emails, clearing desk space, responding to meeting requests... go on, just get them done! Irrespective of their scale, urgency or apparent relevance.

You may be surprised at how much you can achieve. And you may also be very surprised to find that instead of being tiring, it is extremely energising and liberating to act in this way. Once momentum begins, the bigger picture almost always comes more clearly into view.

12

PAUSE

> "The right word may be effective, but no word was ever as effective as a rightly timed pause."
>
> Mark Twain (1835–1910)

In contrast to the earlier Sprint Simple Note, this note discusses the opposite.

Pause.

Like many of the people I work with, you too may be experiencing an increase in the demands on your time and for speedier decision-making, as well as being presented with increasing distractions, options and alternatives. Put simply, there's a lot going on for everyone. We have created situations that call for us to be alert and switched-on all day long.

Your default strategy soon becomes 'press on through': getting whatever needs to be done, done. Some important stuff gets put off (perhaps requiring *celeritas* time to do them) and your attitude and activity becomes tensely charged, frantic, even erratic. This can develop into that unwanted state of being overwhelmed and in extreme cases, into pointlessness.

How many of these apply to you?

- Clutter has increased in and around your workplace.
- You are double-tasking (emailing while on conference calls, texting whilst driving, etc).
- You take several 'gap' tasks with you wherever you go (even to the loo).
- In any lull you turn to your phone, PDA or laptop screen to check for new emails.
- You get bored quickly in meetings and conversations, wanting to cut to the chase without any preamble or irrelevant dialogue.
- You catch yourself tidying up other people's workplaces (tasks not even on your to-do list).
- You are re-reading difficult or complex emails without taking any action (the information just doesn't seem to register on the first pass).

- You miss or compromise meal times.
- Your concentration on tasks is reduced (it hurts to hold focus).
- You fill silent moments with radio, music, texting, making non-urgent calls (silence and nothing-time feels uncomfortable).
- You are extremely irritable when trapped in circumstances out of your control (for example being stuck in traffic, particularly in an area with no mobile signal).
- Excess fatigue causes you to fall asleep in front of the television in the evenings.

Each of these in isolation is probably excusable and may even be a by-product of you stepping up your productivity during busy times. It is when three or more are combined and occur frequently or even become a new norm that change is needed.

Having admitted (to yourself) that some apply to you, consider how they serve you – or not. What is the impact of that choice? Are you waiting for something to change before you do? Could now be the time for you to take action?

Now is your time to:

Pause.

Take a moment for the incessant energy to slow down, to give you a sense of perspective, to allow a brief overview of what's going on and to re-engage all mental systems. Just a few minutes – that might be all it takes.

A five-minute pause can be immensely valuable. Add another three minutes for each item you ticked on the above list. You will find your first pause difficult as you itch to get back into full-on 'doing' mode. But hold on to your pause moment – the benefits will be worth it.

Try this:

1. Sit quietly in an uninterruptable clutter-free place. If one doesn't exist, that's the first place to start: create one.
2. Become aware of tension points around your body (neck, shoulders, face) and allow yourself to switch them off. Say it aloud and experience that tense muscle loosening.
3. Breathe deeply and slowly, six to 10 times. This will accelerate your ability to relax.
4. As soon you catch yourself going into action-related thoughts, release them on the agreement (with yourself!) that you will pick them up again in a few moments.

When you're done, press 'play' again.

13

CLEAR THE CLUTTER

> "The man who removes a mountain begins by carrying away small stones."
>
> **A Chinese proverb**

The build up of clutter is a common early indicator that you have lots going on or you are disorganised – or both. The truth is, it is essentially the same thing.

It is often said that your workspace is a reflection of your headspace – worryingly true for many of us. As if to prove it, the opposite can also be true: a clear desk space makes it easier to be more creative and productive. If you dispute that, you're in denial. Not denial that you can be productive in clutter, but denial that you have enormous potential on the other side of your current chaos.

During work experience week back in 1983 at National Panasonic in Slough, the visiting senior management wanted to see desks with one document and one pen on top, and nothing else other than the studious employee at work with both. Now this may be a touch idealistic, but it is a great call, which I make to you now:

Get everything off your desk that you haven't touched or used in the last 24 hours.

Then try this 33 : 33 : 33 purge that has been successful for me and many of my clients. This can apply to every piece of paper and every email:

- 33% – Keep it. This is the important stuff (the original document maybe). You want to work on it or read it or do something with it soon.
- 33% – Chuck it. This is stuff you've held for too long: old reading material that hasn't been read and won't be. Get rid of it. This includes non-actioned requests that are past their 'please do this' date.
- 33% – Not sure. Box it up and give it to a friend or neighbour on the agreement that, if you don't ask for it back in 2 weeks, they have permission to chuck it out.

That's two-thirds of the clutter cut in one step.

And while you're at it, look again at your workspace right now. What do you see? For me, while writing this note, I can see a rolled up bit of carpet, a box of print cartridges and a chair that never gets sat on. Get them out, NOW.

Enjoy your new space!

14

....

DOUBLE-TASKING

"Do or do not, there is no try."

Yoda

It's a sure sign that you've reached the land of the two Os (overwhelmed and overcommitted) when your productivity engine gets you attempting two or more things at a time. Busy days can see you emailing while on a conference call, attending a meeting while mentally preparing for the next one, and dare I suggest it, texting whilst driving.

Brain science has shown that you can only truly be effective at one conscious task (and that goes for men *and* women!). As soon as you mentally split on more than one, while it appears possible, you will block access to sub-conscious capabilities that could liberate your excellent potential.

Just below the conscious surface, you are busy sensing things: the environment you are in, the sounds, sights, feelings, smells and tastes all around you. These brilliant sensory clues sharpen your ability to know what's going on at a given moment. In addition to this, your amazing brain will be accessing files and information to match the sensory data. Block this channel and you could make mistakes, making you *less* effective, not *more*. You'll miss the nuance in a message, you'll get caught unawares and your ability to communicate (sensing, listening and talking) will be impaired. Try this three-step plan:

Step One – STOP DOING IT! – it's just not worth it; you won't be at your best and the assumed extra productivity is never realised.

Step Two – when you catch yourself double-tasking, laugh at yourself. This is a much more empowering starting point than haranguing or damaging self-talk and it gives you a moment to decide which task this moment calls for. Decide, do it and drop the other.

Step Three – A double-tasking urge is a call to pause. Take five minutes to follow the Pause Simple Note and return to the task/s. Have a look at the next two to three hours in your schedule and carve out the time to complete the competing task.

You don't get double brilliance by double-tasking, but more likely half and half.

Enjoy the comparative ease and liberation of working on one conscious task, brilliantly. You are incredible at your best, so try and be in that place as often as you can, one step at a time.

15

BLACKBERRY MOMENTS

> "Our doubts are traitors, and make us lose the good we oft might win, by fearing to attempt."
>
> William Shakespeare (1564–1616)

Overwhelm is present or looming nearby when you begin turning every moment into a BlackBerry (or iPhone, PDA, mobile phone, etc.) moment.

Mobile technology now enables us to always be 'switched on' and connected with colleagues, customers, friends, information sources, news, data streams... everything, 24 hours a day.

This is neither a good thing, nor a bad thing. It's just a thing.

When the unspoken thought in your head is constantly 'I'm so busy', then you may unsurprisingly create a habit of turning to your phone or mobile device in every gap, convincing yourself that this is a natural extension of your effectiveness. It is almost laughable that when I have caught myself in this state, I am often synchronising my mobile, even though it does it on its own every 15 minutes. I'm hurrying up new information rather than appreciating and enjoying a moment of silence!

This will become unhelpful – you are confusing this constant connection with inspired action. It is not *in*spired; it is *ex*pired, in that the motivation for action comes from outside of us. You are not your phone and it is not an extension of you.

I developed *Top 10 Tips for Email Mastery*, which can be found at simontyler.com and in the Conquering the Email Dragon Simple Note. The tips can really support change; in short they include noticing that we are treating every email as urgent, as if they were telephone calls (the audible or visual prompt saying 'answer me!'). Eventually your sense of urgency becomes so overloaded that you have no time for and cannot even recognise the important stuff.

A pause is needed – things are not going to change without you being actively involved. This sounds obvious but it's true. Any change will feel uncomfortable – as you shift an ingrained habit, you will feel the strength of the habit pulling you back to your mobile again and again. Know that this is just the habit playing out, not your choice and not the best thing to do. Be strong.

Here are a few changes for you to consider:

- Extend the download frequency to four times as long as you have it set currently (for me moving from every 15 minutes to every hour made me super-conscious of the poor habit I was in – I laughed each time I went to my phone ready to download again, but stopping just in time until eventually the new habit was formed).
- Leave your phone on its own, away from you, for 24 hours (sounds easy, but I seriously dare you to try it – this is a powerful habit-breaker and you will experience pangs during the 24-hour freedom period).
- Try a TLA – 'Technology Liberation Alternator' – an hour fully connected, an hour without, an hour on, an hour off, and be brilliant in each of the phases, making the most of each).
- Become a single taskmaster by switching your device off when you are in a meeting, working on an assignment, writing copy, whatever. Not just onto silent, make sure it's fully off. Then turn it on when you are done and become that master communicator again.

Find the strength and see it through.

16

RESETTING YOUR DAILY DEFAULT MODE

> "The last of the human freedoms — to choose one's attitude in any given set of circumstances, to choose one's own way."
>
> Viktor Frankl (1905–1997)

Much has been written about the number of thoughts we have every day (something in the order of sixty thousand) and that most of them are broadly the same as the previous day's. What I take from this statistic is that our plans for change and personal evolution tend to develop slowly, certainly slower than is possible with a little focused intent.

Some of my personal development work in 2010 with my coach, Drew Rozell, focused on my thoughts: specifically, shifting from a hands-off way of accepting whatever they might be, to consciously and actively choosing them, and noticing the impact they had on subsequent thoughts and, ultimately, on the results I created.

What I discovered in the process, or rather, what I *remembered* in the process, is that the first hours in the day are exponentially more significant than trying to think of positive change, developmental and corrective stuff in later hours.

Every morning, between waking up and your first appointment, you are collecting your thoughts. These regular pattern-thoughts are normally sourced from three places: yesterday's events, today's expected events and from the story you repeat about your current habitual circumstance (e.g. I never have enough time', 'there's too much to do', etc). These stories become your default setting and subsequent thoughts can only ever be linked to them. It is your thought starting point; which is not necessarily a great place and one that requires a lot of effort and massive positive luck to shift upwards. Hence change happens slowly.

What might your recurring story be? Is it the setting that helps you evolve or does it keep you where you are?

The great news is you can change your default, and that is my challenge in this note. Begin each day with a resetting. Choose a time (same each day), such as just after you brush your teeth. It's important that you think of something you believe, not an outrageous pipe-dream thought. Make it positive, such as 'I'll use the time I have today brilliantly', 'I'll focus my time only on high-importance things today' or 'I have resources available to me all day long'. Choose a statement that feels best to you.

Changing your morning thinking and setting more powerful intentions for the day can be the distinction between achievers and non-achievers, the evolved and the unevolved, the relaxed and the stressed. Work with a coach on this; it will be worth it.

17

TIME AND SPACE

> "It does not matter how slowly you go, so long as you do not stop."
>
> Confucius (551–479 BC)

Time is a precious commodity. We talk about it constantly: Find time, save time, not enough time, it's time for… One might even say we have become obsessed by it. I have caught myself inadvertently using time as a pressure device to get things done (leaving things till the last minute), then changing my physical state because of the lack of it, setting myself up for stress in the belief that time is my only motivator.

Addiction to time manifests itself in a number of ways. When you become addicted, time-management training courses will have little or no effect, as it (time) is managing you. Could any of the following personas be you?

The Clock Watcher – Glancing at clocks or your watch, powering up your mobile phone to check the time, not trusting yourself to know the actual time or the elapsed time – this often means you are under constant tension, waiting to move. This is extremely draining!

The Gap Filler – Looking for gaps in your diary and filling them with meetings. Or, worse still, knowing there are unallocated gaps and allowing your current stuff (meetings, checking emails, writing what should be a straight-forward letter) to magically expand to fill them.

The Fast Mover – not in a smooth, athletic way but in a more frantic, jittery and erratic way (this can be linked to you trying to process too much at once).

The Reduced Attention Spanner – you're double-thinking, wanting to move on to the next thing before fully completing the first task and thus missing the feeling of progress and subtleties in relationships, etc.

The Commitment Avoider – the thought of agreeing to that meeting/workshop/programme just seems ridiculous. You think, 'Where am I going to find the time?', and before you know it, you're missing out on enjoyable, fun or developmental opportunities because you're still caught in the mix of the small, seemingly important (but not really) stuff.

I have coached many executives who find themselves playing out one or more of these roles and I have delivered various time-management training courses over the years and each time, it just confirms the fact that *it's not about time!*

While there are deeper things to work on (with a coach), I have noticed the direct link between **TIME** and **SPACE**. I'm not introducing Doctor Who and his TARDIS here. Instead, here is something much more practical.

The spaces in which you exist have a direct link to the relationship you have with time. Change one and you will magically increase the other.

My challenge to you as part of this Simple Note is to create space:

- In your schedule – just create a blank, and fill it with nothing.
- In your workspace – clear your desk; empty a drawer; clear the area around your meeting or other seating areas.

- In your mind – complete tasks (mentally if not physically); sit quietly for 10 minutes (read other Simple Notes to evolve your ability to 'pause' brilliantly).
- Find some (physical) space and spend some time there – maybe outdoors, or hold your meeting in a room too big for the participants; perhaps work in a large room on your own – I particularly like this mini tip as it always delivers a new result, just try it and see. The opposite is also true: small, crowded meeting rooms are more likely to create tense, clipped conversations and the agenda slips and the meetings tend to overrun.
- Become aware of the spaces you are in; explore ways to expand the space around you; shift away from confinement.

You will feel the resistance of your ego still wanting to panic about time as you begin kicking your addiction. Keep going. You'll be delighted with what shows up.

18

MOVING ON

> "All you have to do is look straight and see the road, and when you see it, don't sit looking at it – walk."
>
> Ayn Rand (1905–1982)

As you make your way through life and encounter tough times and difficult choices, elders may often remind you that 'things are sent to try us'. In many ways they were masterful at carrying these trials and suffering with them for years, even for lifetimes. However, remember that rather than just bearing the load, exploring and expanding your potential is your right and your journey.

I notice the distinction between people who are tolerating stuff and those who do not. There is an amazing difference in what the latter achieve and how much they seem able to enjoy themselves, be more fully present and at their best.

Consider times in your career when you have moved the fastest, achieved more and made connections with little effort. Compare that to the times when it's been hard work, you're grinding your teeth in frustration and what you need seems always out of reach.

There is a link between these two states and the amount that you are 'putting up' with. Right now, what are you tolerating or suffering or just plain fed up with?

You have two choices:

1. Change it.
2. Change your attitude to it.

Change It – actually change your situation; engage in thoughts and conversation about options. Let go of it, step away and release it. You will learn more from letting go than trying to eventually solve these conundrums. The movement of energy and the vacuum you create will be filled with new people, opportunities and challenges.

If you're not yet ready for change, then your alternate option is to:

Change your attitude to the problem – not flippantly, nor with a barrage of unconvincing self-talk. No, I mean a real attitude shift (it's sometimes best to work with a colleague or coach on this one). What are the good things about the situation? What are you giving? What are you getting? What are you learning? What more is there to learn? How could this be the most powerful experience for you?

There is a third 'choice', and it's the one most people unconsciously take: The 'put up with it' option. However, this is not actually a choice – it doesn't work, you cannot and do not actually 'put' it anywhere. It will almost immediately have a mental, physical and emotional impact on your potential and your power.

Carry too many of these and you may become irritable, find it difficult to relax or concentrate, begrudge certain tasks or people and complete them less than brilliantly. Add days or weeks to this and you are simply not going to be in a good place.

A great coaching approach that I work on with clients from time to time is Thomas Leonard's (Coachville) Toleration Free Programme. It is a focused way of zapping the irritators and eliminating elements of your life that drain you. Sometimes though you may find yourself in situations where a bigger decision is required.

When the situation you have been putting up with begins to take up more of your thinking or irritates or drains you in any way, the choice remains: Change it or change your attitude to it.

'If you don't like something change it. If you can't change it, change your attitude. Don't complain.'

Maya Angelou, poet and civil rights activist

19

BOOST YOUR ENERGY

> "Energy and persistence conquer all things."
>
> Benjamin Franklin (1706–1790)

Much of my work with individuals and teams over the last 10 years has involved working with behavioural and attitude assessments, helping my clients understand how they, and those around them, are wired. Knowing one's self is the only place to begin.

You have a unique make-up and combination of motivators, stressors and natural and learnt ways of coping. When the going gets tough and your workload increases, with growing expectations (and lesser time) you will experience a physical response that you may often ignore, patch over or simply cope with and never resolve.

My wish for you is that you always have the energy you need and that you operate at your best as much of the time as you can. Your energy, which fuels your attitude, is the most powerful tool within your control. If you are deficient in an area on which your make-up thrives you will become drained.

From the following list, establish what relieves and re-energises you. Notice the opposites too and the damage silently sapping your power. You will need a combination of:

Physical exercise – even when you feel mentally or emotionally drained and time does not offer the obvious opportunity, exercise could be exactly what's needed. This could be a run, a competitive game, a swim or a brisk walk. Many who need this form of energy boost often opt for the opposite: vegging out. No energy is gained.

Socialising – spending time in conversation with friends or colleagues with no agendas, no timetables, no expectations. Those of us who feed on this form of energy boost often opt for the opposite: work harder, being alone, pressing on. No energy is gained.

Chill-out time – engage in stuff with no pressure: TV, reading, music, activities where the pressure is off and are a buffer zone from the everyday chaos. Those of us who feed on this energy boost often opt for the opposite: staying busy, working longer and focusing on producing, producing, producing. No energy is gained.

Solitary – spend time alone, perhaps with selected music but often in silence, walking away from the hubbub. Those of us who feed on this energy boost often opt to stay in the hubbub to get more done, to work it out, to find out more. Again, no energy gained.

Treat yourself to a sample of each of the four types over the next week and evaluate which one (or more) delivers the most clear and clean boost. Then commit to including a proper dose each week. You will notice the difference to your thinking, your sense of priorities, clarity and ability to relax, to be creative and to work faster.

20

SIMPLIFY YOUR OVERWHELM

> "Simplicity is the ultimate sophistication."
>
> **Leonardo da Vinci (1452–1519)**

Most of the people I coach, myself included, experience overwhelm at some time or another. Do you?

There is a lot going on. Even if your company isn't going through a merger, acquisition or other significant strategic change, the chances are that at some time or another everything has become labelled as urgent. Meetings are habitually scheduled that you simply *have* to attend. There is always information being created that you simply *have* to absorb. Projects are multiplying. Departments and responsibilities are being merged, and the details still *have* to be picked up and worked through.

This is where over*whelm* becomes over*load*, and ultimately, over!

A former coaching client asked me to help her adjust her attitude to the overwhelm she was experiencing. She was ready to take a different approach to the pointless and ineffective 'work longer' approach. The dictionary definition of 'overwhelm' provoked my thinking.

1. Overwhelm is 'to be submerged'.

Being submerged means oxygen can be restricted. You need to breathe. When you experience overwhelm it causes shortening of breath, tightening of the chest and hunching (perhaps over the desk and keyboard). You are reducing the flow of air. This seriously changes your physiology and reduces your productivity and ability to think creatively and freely, as the brain begins shifting to survival mode and shutting down non-essential services.

When submerged, install breathing apparatus. Set an alarm or some kind of reminder to pause every 15 minutes and take five to 10 deep inhalations and slow exhalations. You WILL notice the difference.

Also consider installing a periscope – when submerged, the immediate environment is all you can see, and even then it may be obscured. A periscope gives instant height and long sight. Change your position (stand up), go talk to someone and take two minutes to consider where you are, what you've achieved in the day so far and what is now most important.

2. Overwhelm is 'to be weighed down'.

When new weights are added to a system or a person without any change, there is a displacement of energy or strain. This needs to go somewhere and can manifest itself, ironically, as a 'snap'. The weights (or overwhelm items) are still there but are no longer supported and have become scattered. People then go at the scattered pile of tasks in a haphazard way, making no real impression on the original volume but becoming busy and exhausted on the way.

There are a number of ways I have been able to help individuals and teams increase their capacity in corporate life without extending (sometimes even reducing) the hours they work. It takes guts to pause, step back and simplify the situation.

To support more weight a bar needs to be strengthened. For you it means going beyond the obvious need for delegation, prioritisation and elimination. This means taking some personal care actions: rest, refuelling, relaxation, fitness development. Matching what needs to be done with those around you who are more efficient at doing those particular things is a no-brainer, but matching yourself with the tasks and situations to which you are naturally aligned is of equal importance.

21

THREE SIMPLE STEPS TO SOMEWHERE

"Most people never run far enough on their first wind to find out if they've got a second. Give your dreams all you've got and you'll be amazed at the energy that comes out of you."

William James (1842–1910)

It will sound obvious and you will agree, intellectually at least, that getting somewhere essentially involves three steps:

1. Deciding where you want to go.
2. Realising where you are now.
3. Setting off.

Your personal and business circumstances may often become so busy that you slip into a 'merely existing' mode. In this mode you are just getting things done, but not actually moving consistently in any one direction. And you may also be pretty good at justifying the situation: 'I'll sort it out in the next gap…', 'It'll be alright when…', 'This is my job, life is like this…'

A phrase I am perhaps guilty of over-using in my workshops and speaking events is the call to action: 'Nothing Changes Unless Something Changes'. If you don't take some kind of new action, you'll be stuck in a version of today's mire in two months or maybe even two years.

In this note I would like to draw your attention to step one:

1. Deciding where you want to go.

This crucial question can take time and focus to answer and it's really difficult to do it alone (get a coach). The more work you put in here, the faster you will move towards your goal.

If you are going to embark on this alone, consider carving out 30 minutes this week and go somewhere where you won't be disturbed. For the first 15 minutes, simply write about what success means to you.

Some examples include:

1. Freedom of time.
2. Spending freedom.
3. Space (to live, move, write, relax, etc).
4. Flow of income.
5. Life is organised around you.
6. Hassle-free.
7. Doing what you enjoy and are good at.

For the second 15 minutes relax into the chair, and let your mind go to the place you have just described, where you are enjoying all that success. As you conclude your meeting, note down any additional insights you may have had, fold the paper, file it and let go of the whole experience.

Do the same thing one week later, with a new sheet of paper.

And, if you're up for it, repeat a third time another week later. You will, by now, have clarity and have initiated an unstoppable wave of change-thinking that will take you towards your more clearly-defined destination.

22

URGENTIA

> "Act as if what you do makes a difference.
> It does."
>
> William James (1842–1910)

When evaluating your tasks, intentions, goals and to-do lists etc., the Eisenhower Method is a trusty and well-used maxim applied in almost every time-management lesson or programme. I'm sure you know it and can recite the points it seeks to make.

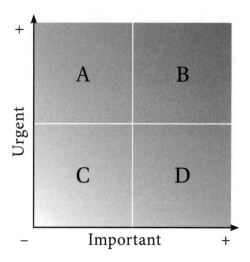

I'll remind you:

Identify all the tasks, commitments and actions in which you are involved and categorise them into the four boxes in the diagram above.

Assess the degree to which they are urgent (looming deadline or immediate requirement to be completed) and the degree to which they are important (developing and evolving yourself, solving bigger challenges, leading to your goals or greater success).

The best practice principle is to:

Work on the Urgent and Important first (*Box B*).

Work on the Not Urgent and Important box second (*Box D*).

Handle the Urgent, Unimportant in new ways (*Box A*).

Avoid Box C.

This 2×2 method comes into most of my coaching conversations. With today's constant volume of requests, emails, meetings, projects, new possibilities, distractions, games, texts and social networking, people commonly but unknowingly drift into a state of 'Urgentia'.

Urgentia is my word to describe a loss of awareness of actual important thinking and actions. Instead, everything that grabs your focus is laced with unspecified urgency.

Extreme Urgentia is where your days have become full of a mixed dose of unimportant distractions. Things that aren't important simply aren't important. Ideally you shouldn't spend excessive time (perhaps worth specifically defining what 'excessive' might be for you) on them. Your evolved self should eliminate them entirely.

In today's busy environment, we are constantly told that everything is now in Box B (Urgent and Important). Most of the time this is not actually true. What may have happened, without you or those around you being consciously aware of it, is that you have become addicted to Urgent. You are suffering from 'Urgentia'.

Your many electronic devices are, by their nature, urgent. These include phones, especially mobiles, texts (even more so), email, instant message alerts and so on. Add to this the natural urgency of media (TV, radio, newspapers) and the adverts that scream for your immediate attention and action and it isn't surprising that we now have an environment in which urgency rules. These are almost all in dangerous Box A (the urgency masks the fact that they are absolutely unimportant).

Today you have more choices available to you than ever before – you are capable of taking empowered self-development steps. Changing your business and personal life dramatically is a real and attainable option. But we often don't. These actions are always important and not urgent (precious Box D). They don't shout and scream; they require you to be conscious and deliberate. Time spent here ALWAYS pays back, but it is lost to the urgency lists.

Box D enjoys only fleeting moments of attention as your diary fills with the urgent stuff. And without noticing, you are caught idling in Box C, convincing yourself that what you are doing is important when really it isn't. It's simply not urgent and you have been enjoying the non-urgency of it. The same relaxed option awaits you in the important Box D – as soon as you focus on it and do it!

Urgentia is not big or clever, even though it feels that way when we are caught up in it. Bizarrely, when people are in the state of Urgentia, they appear more important than those working on the important! Urgentia leads to missed goals, slipped deadlines, excessive stress and anxiety and the feeling of no progress despite what seems to be immense effort.

What's a simple way to cure Urgentia?

Start an audit this week of how and where you have spent your time. Broadly mark against each period or task where it fell in the diagram shown above.

Ask yourself the question: "Was this task truly important to me, my goals and aspirations?" Begin again, deliberately. Handle the urgent and do the important. Book time, reserve the space and take whatever action moves you forward in the direction of your goals.

Be deliberate and purposeful in carving out time and space to focus on an important but not urgent item. It *will* meet resistance, but see it through.

23

....

SIX OF ONE, HALF A DOZEN
OF THE OTHER

> "Nothing will ever be attempted if all possible objections must be first overcome."
>
> Samuel Johnson (1709–1784)

The expression in the title is one of many that invite you to maintain a balanced view of a situation. So, on the basis of my profound belief that your journey through life is as much about remembering as it is about learning new things, I shall bring the phrase back into your focus.

Let me start with the assertion that when you think the world or a certain context is against you, then it probably is. You feel less powerful and less positive. You are more likely to be tense for longer periods of time. You smile less, frown more, grit your teeth and sit hunched up. You are more reluctant to change anything. And perhaps most noticeably, you over-react to situations, often inappropriately.

On the opposite side of the equation, if you think that the world or your context is absolutely ideal, then it probably is. You feel powerful, positive, confident, expanding. You allow yourself to relax deeply and often. You smile all the time, walk taller and see more. You are willing to change anything and are open to new thinking. And perhaps most noticeably, you allow situations to be what they are, and consider and respond to them appropriately. There is no resistance.

Whatever is happening for you right now – at home, at work or simply inside you – just is. There will be 'six of one, half a dozen of the other', and you get to decide which half grabs your attention.

Over my coaching years, it has become abundantly clear among my clients which of the two states allows them to achieve more, transform and transition faster, and wear a fabulous grin.

The pragmatically powerful 'six of one...' quote is a reminder to nudge your thinking towards a more helpful state. When you are noticing only the wrong six, it compounds, and more than six seem to turn up to prove it. Seek the other six, and simplify your situation in that moment.

For the next week I challenge you to notice your state, and on the occasions when you are facing the not-so-nice-six, ask yourself and write down the answers to the following:

1. What could be the 'half a dozen of the other' here?
2. What might be/could be good about this?
3. How might this be helpful for me or others?

Keep asking the same questions until something comes to mind, in even the toughest situations.

24

....

TOLERATIONS

> "It isn't the mountain ahead that wears you out – it's the grain of sand in your shoe."
>
> Robert Service (1874–1958)

One of the first things that I address when working with coaching clients is their energy levels. I aim to move their levels consistently higher, and one of the fastest and most sustainable ways of doing this is through clearing energy drains.

Tolerations are all those annoying, aggravating, frustrating, energy-draining things that you are tolerating, putting up with or suffering. They drain time, money, other resources, love, patience and so on. They take up space and eat up your energy. When your toleration count is high, your energy levels are frequently low, your enthusiasm wanes quickly, your resilience is low and everyday challenges hit you too hard.

All these tolerations can come from the behaviour of others, unforeseen situations, unmet needs, crossed boundaries, loose ends and unfinished past business, frustrations, problems and even your own behaviour.

They could include a cluttered desk, family members who do not respect your decisions, clients who don't pay on time, a dripping tap that annoys you or even a door that sticks in the frame. And if that tap has been dripping or that door has been sticking for months or even years it has a direct (and negative) link to your ability to feel good.

You may even have repeatedly told yourself that these things are just part of your life and there's no point paying any attention to them as they're not quite at the point where you *have* to do something about them, and thus you just get on with the rest of your stuff.

The wonderful thing is that there is an opportunity for you to gain huge boosts to your energy, productivity and general 'feel good' state, by following a gentle process of becoming toleration-free.

Simply recognise that tolerations exist and begin to eliminate as many as possible. By sweeping these away, your path to reaching your goals will become clearer and easier to traverse.

Step One – write down everything that you are currently tolerating. Common areas where these show up are in our homes (the various rooms in which you spend time), with our family and environment around us and in our work life and situations. Keep adding to this list as you think of the tolerations in your life.

Step Two – start sweeping them away, one at a time. Begin with the easy ones. If you get stuck, get support from your coach or a close friend or colleague.

To get you in motion, I challenge you to start that list right now and then pick three from your list (easy ones first, to create some momentum) and wipe them out. You'll feel so energised by doing so that you'll carry on, well on your way to becoming toleration-free!

25

INSTANT LIBERATION

> "It is not the strongest of the species that survive, nor the most intelligent, but the one most responsive to change."
>
> Charles Darwin (1809–1882)

When encountering overwhelm again I recalled a phrase I once read: *"Possessions you cannot give away end up possessing you"*, and as I sat in my thinking chair I stared at the cupboard full of books – some read, some not. Books from my past, books I was holding onto, just in case I needed to refer to them or perhaps even may read again; books for the future, already purchased and ready to be picked up. The shelves were sagging under their weight. In my mind I was experiencing the same.

So out they all came, with most going straight into a box for the charity shop. I kept only twelve.

The feeling was incredibly liberating and gave me an amazing energy boost for several days. The energy powered new momentum to make other, much delayed changes and to get sorted, which now seemed so much easier to take on.

I challenge you to take a new look around the places you spend most of your time and let go, pass on or recycle things that no longer have anything to do with the you of today.

Here's wishing you an energy-filled step to simplicity.

26

BRINGING GOALS TO LIFE

"The problems of this world cannot possibly be solved by sceptics or cynics whose horizons are limited by the obvious realities. We need men who can dream of things that never were."

John F. Kennedy (1917–1963)

At some time in your career you will have been told that you should use goals to drive you to new results, raise your game or capitalise on your potential. It's no surprise then, that there are hundreds of 'Goal-Getter' or 'Goal-Maker' products, processes, programmes and coaching supports to help us.

I have often spent time thinking about my goals. Do I actually have any? What was my route to get what I now have – was it goal-fuelled? To be honest my answers were inconclusive, so I set about simplifying them, which is my way through such situations.

Put simply, goals come to life when the following mental states exist:

Clarity – I am clear about them.

Belief – I believe I will achieve (even if they are a stretch or seemingly impossible).

Action – I act as if they have come about already.

Perhaps you have only one or two of these steps in place and the other/s are low or non-existent. It doesn't mean the goal won't be achieved, merely that it may take longer, or be achieved with less clarity.

Score each of the three mental states from one to 10 and multiply the result. The range then is from one to one thousand.

Where a score is zero, the obvious result is always zero (it will not be achieved) no matter how high the other states may be.

Where the scores are low, work in just one of the mental state areas, not necessarily all three. This can speed up your journey.

My scores have often been low in clarity, always high in belief and variable in action. Any enhancements I make simply accelerate things for me.

27

EXPECTATION PLAYLIST

> "Do not spoil what you have by desiring what you have not; remember that what you now have was once among the things you only hoped for."
>
> Epicurus (341–270 BC)

In a coaching call I invited a client to talk to me as if from the end of the week, looking back.

Immediately, she described an expected set of outcomes that she knew, in advance, that she wouldn't feel great about. Reality was informing her range of results and feelings. But she had a choice. It was only Tuesday, four full working days to go before that Friday outcome. What would she like to say? What feelings would she want to have, given the choice?

In spite of the apparent reality of what might occur she began to describe a new expectation.

When we caught up a week later, the result was indeed different, not her initial expectation but better, improved and just as she had set the desired outcome, she enjoyed a feeling of contentment and success that were definitely not on the first agenda.

Does this happen to you? Of course it does, perhaps more often than you realise. You are rolling towards a set of outcomes and resulting feelings; an unconscious but just as powerful expectation. Your mood and attitudes are pre-determined, like a DJ who has already chosen the playlist before the programme begins. Your expectations will come to pass unless you change the playlist.

Start with thinking about your default expectation, then upgrade it in spite of reality. Remind yourself daily and your attitude muscles will do the rest.

28

RETREAT

> "Nothing is a waste of time if you use the
> experience wisely."
>
> Auguste Rodin (1840–1917)

The double, almost contrasting, meaning of the word retreat is worthy of investigation.

To retreat is to go back, reverse or return. It also refers to an escape, a time away from everyday hustle and bustle to reflect and review.

When I meet with tough circumstances and it feels like I am wading through mud, one of my first actions is to press on, try harder, work longer and throw more at it. In the past, this has led to an energy and fun-sapping time and I just don't like it.

My challenge to you is to consider where you are encountering resistance. What seems heavy-going or hard work? Then *retreat* – go back in the other direction, take time to reflect or simply take a completely different route.

Keep yourself in that retreated position for a period of time (an hour or more) and review as much about your current situation as you can:

- How did I get here?
- What or where is it easy/difficult/meeting resistance?
- Who has experience here?
- What other options are available to me (given abundant time or money)?

Shake yourself off and return to your challenge. You will have had or set in motion new insights and thinking to shift gears.

29

BECOME FRUSTRATION-FREE

> "Everything that irritates us about others can lead us to an understanding of ourselves."
>
> Carl Jung (1875–1961)

You're a busy person. There is a lot happening in your life; communication is fast and comes from multiple sources. The everyday choices about where to focus and what gets done seem to multiply.

Increasingly, the ability to get things done relies on your connection and collaboration with others who experience the same plethora of options and make completely different decisions from yours.

Outcome = frustration.

Frustration with yourself and the choices you did or didn't make. Frustration with the situations and contexts in which you find yourself. And frustration with others for all of those reasons too.

I held consecutive meetings with two long-standing coaching clients, who shared similar but different stories of their frustration. I noticed again how frustration quickly affects your attitude and mood and sets up an expectation of more frustration. You feel drained, even angry and bitter at times and it just doesn't feel good.

I have continually proved to myself (and to a lot of clients) that when you feel good you perform better, think faster, more creatively and attract more opportunities and desirable events (which make you feel good!). So my challenge to ease past your frustration is to shift to a more empowered state.

Here's a method you can immediately use to neutralise your frustrations.

Grab a pen, find a new page in the back of your notebook and write down on the left hand side the top five things that are frustrating you. Just the frustration, not the why.

Alongside each, begin a new sentence using the same subject description replacing 'frustrated by' with 'it's great that' and allow your creative brain to come up with the reasons why the situation is great.

How does it work? It shifts your mood and attitude to

at least neutral; from there you will feel better, release more of your creative thinking power and probably come up with more compelling reasons why things are okay. Choose the serene response.

And to be frustration-free?

First, give yourself clear and unambiguous permission to be free of frustration (you may be addicted to it).

Second, stop talking about your frustrations (in effect fuelling them and bringing them to life).

Third, keep working with the neutraliser method.

30

BOOST PERSONAL PRODUCTIVITY

> "The more efficient a force is, the more silent and the more subtle it is."
>
> Mahatma Gandhi (1869–1948)

Many of my clients find themselves in the middle of significantly increased numbers of To-Do lists. The projects in which they are involved are increasing but the availability of resources remains stagnant.

Perhaps you too have found yourself in such a situation, feeling the pressure to achieve and complete more. Yet the distractions are many, the number of meetings multiply and unanswered messages mount up.

The real productive progress many make is, at best, partial.

Here is a simple tip to boost your productivity. For the next two weeks take the following action steps at the start of your working day (and I repeat the importance of the start rather than the middle or end, as you are setting in motion some crucial attitude shifts).

Pause for 10 minutes, i.e. sit at rest with no distractions.

Of all the things you have to do, think about which three things (no more, no less) you would really like to progress or complete today (they don't even have to be deadline-dependent).

Write them down on the back of one of your business cards and keep this card with you all day.

This card is your absolute focus. Irrespective of the meetings in your schedule, the calls you make or take, the three things on the card are your purpose for the day. Your day is not over till they are done. If you complete them early (and do not resist that happening), enjoy the rest of the day in a relaxed state of 'completion'. Anything else you get done is purely a bonus.

Repeat for a concerted period of time (minimum 10 working days, maximum 20). You will have completed between 30 and 60 significant productivity steps, and I am convinced you would not achieve this number without this sort of focus. You will otherwise be at the beck and call of everyday tasks, demands and miscellaneous distractions that may not have any impact on your important personal productivity.

31

DOWNWIND

> "The fishermen know that the sea is dangerous and the storm terrible, but they have never found these dangers sufficient reason for remaining ashore."
>
> Vincent van Gogh (1853–1890)

After returning from a week's sailing in the Baltic, I was full of stories and analogies and ready to dispense them liberally.

One parallel that struck me clearly on this particular trip was the challenge of working with the direction of the wind and how it affects the route to your destination.

It is rare in life and rarer at sea to simply select a destination and head in a straight line towards it. Fluctuating conditions, just like those you experience in your workplace, mean that a straight line is not an option. If you simply press on, you will feel like you are moving only slowly, if at all, towards your goal. You may have to adjust both your sails and your course.

On one particular day in the Baltic, heading to our destination would have meant having the wind directly behind us. This sounds swell and fast, doesn't it? Just fill the sails and off we go in a straight line. It can be fast but in truth this is a dangerous 'point-of-sail' and difficult for the boat to maintain safely, as the wind in the tail puts immense strain on the sails, the mast and the potential widow-making boom. The preferred setting was away from the wind, extending our journey in distance but using the sailboat more efficiently, safely and yet still maintaining speed.

How often do the conditions in your world seem absolutely perfect (i.e. the wind is behind you) but the experience becomes nerve-wracking with things happening so fast around you? The reckless stay on that course and often attract damage – to relationships, to projects, to workloads and to quality. The worried turn completely off course and avoid the conditions completely, slowing right down and missing the opportunity for growth, improvement, change or project progress.

The most powerful choice would be to adjust your course slightly, in effect to tack left and right. At work this might be in the form of a rapid review of your short and long-term goals.

Could they move or be different, or even be put on hold?

What might now be in range?

Perhaps set some short-term goals that you would not normally consider, and install more frequent rapid reviews and re-evaluations of the situation, your speed and progress. Pause (see the Pause Simple Note) and tune in to your intuition. It may also mean shifting roles within the team for a few weeks, changing the focus and challenging ingrained habits.

Whatever the conditions for you in the weeks ahead, consider where you are heading and where the wind is coming from or taking you. What short-term changes could you make to maximise your safety, enjoyment and results?

32

HOW TEAMS CAN ACHIEVE
FIVE OUT OF FIVE

"Treat people as if they were what they ought to be, and you help them to become what they are capable of being."

Johann Wolfgang von Goethe (1749–1832)

While working with a team of talented, motivated and busy project managers, I was absorbed by a regular part of their team meetings – a 'temperature check'. Each team member was invited to rate how they felt in terms of connection to the team, current happiness level etc., and allocate those feelings a score out of five.

Somewhat predictably, the scores ranged from two (the

person who was swamped in projects) through assured threes and a four (the optimist who just loves the challenge).

I took this opportunity to pose the silly question of what a five might be.

The answers were interesting and began to unlock the possibility that a five might actually exist. Each team member viewed a 'five' situation quite differently. For some it was about a sense of completion, for others it was recognition, noticeable impact, smiling more, learning, connecting, celebrating and so on. Much of the criteria for a score of five was off the agenda and considered out of reach. No surprise then that no one considered having a five-out-of-five experience.

I even sensed a hint of guilt about the thought of letting oneself experience an indulgent five (and any other inappropriate adjectives). How ridiculous. I go to work seeking five-out-of-five days and many of the most successful people with whom I have worked have more five-days than any other number.

Is it simply a shift of mindset? Perhaps.

In order to move this particular team on and continue to open up the possibility of a five in their lives it was time to simplify.

Rather than create a vision of a five-day, how about a five-out-of-five moment or hour or morning? What might the circumstances be? We worked through a few questions and came up with a personal recipe for each member of the team.

So my challenge to you is to consider the possibility of a five-out-of-five day in your world. It needs to start well and be focused on what leads you to that five feeling.

Consider:
- How you would start that day?
- What would you focus on first?
- Who would you spend time with?
- What or who would you avoid?

Go on, simplify and create some five-out-of-five experiences, string them together and soon entire days will feel great.

33

THOUGHT MANAGEMENT 101

"The soul is dyed the colour of its thoughts. Think only on those things that are in line with your principles and can bear the light of day. The content of your character is your choice. Day by day, what you do is who you become."

Heraclitus (535–475 BC)

Have you ever wondered why you think what you think? And whether there actually is a direct link between what you think about and what turns up in your life?

On my journeys I have met evolved souls who enjoy such a deeply serene place that they can exert incredible control over their thoughts and seem able to create what they want to maintain and sustain their serenity. But if you are still in a thought-evolution phase, controlling your thoughts is a difficult task.

In simple terms, your thoughts are triggered by the plethora of stimuli to which you are exposed. Colours, people, sounds, food, body position, places, smells. Before you begin the hard work of managing all this there is one simple step you can immediately take to improve your results.

Choose the thoughts you want to follow.

Without 'thinking about your thinking' you can find yourself focusing on an ill-desired thought for several minutes. And in doing so you activate the thought, give it life and creative space and your mood and attitude shifts with it.

If you follow a positive thought, you automatically expand it with additional linked thoughts. Your mood and attitude shift that way too.

Which feels better? Which thought, when followed, leads to new positive thoughts, ideas and the ability to notice opportunities that may otherwise have just gone past?

I challenge you to practise this exercise today. When a thought that you don't like comes up, simply let it go. Initiate a new and better thought (like the view from your window or the best thing about your next hour) and follow that for at least two minutes. Then consider how you feel.

And as a bonus to this exercise, consider what thoughts you cause in those around you. Are they positive? What do you cause? What might they be thinking about as a result of you, your actions, words and attitudes?

Keep it simple and follow the good ones.

34

HAVE YOU LEFT A PAN OF MILK ON?

> "Waste not fresh tears over old griefs."
>
> Euripides (480–406 BC)

Have you ever experienced that nagging sensation as you leave home or the office that something important has been left undone?

Whenever my family leaves home for a weekend or on holiday the flippant question, 'Have you left a pan of milk on the boil?' is asked to make us rack our brains to make sure nothing has been forgotten.

I have noticed the energetic drain that this type of uncertainty and incompleteness brings in myself and in my clients.

When your concentration is impaired you act out in uncertain ways, even in tasks in which you should have certainty. This feeling of incompleteness is annoying, uncomfortable and quite simply holding you back.

I have also noticed that the sensation can still be occurring at deeper levels beyond the obvious milk pan situation.

Small, almost forgotten, unfinished items from the immediate past or more distant times gnaw away and reduce your potential to feel great during the day.

These 'incompletes' might be unpaid bills, outstanding conversations or pending decisions, partially-completed projects, gratitude not given or not received and so on. The list can be enormous and somehow our brain holds the disappointment that we cannot just complete them all today.

Assuming you do actually want to feel great and operate at five out of five (see that Simple Note) more often, you have two choices:

1. Say to yourself that whatever is undone is the way it is; you are happy that it is so and you are ready to be fully present now, unaffected by whatever is incomplete. While this is a quick and easy way forward, you probably have an active and investigative mind that may return to scanning your memory banks, thus bringing back these energy-draining items.

2. The second option is to grasp the list and get explicit
    with what is gnawing at you, even (and especially)
    the tiny subtle items. Look at the list and make a
    decision here and now about which can be completed
    immediately, which can go into your diary for the
    week ahead to be knocked off, and which are no longer
    relevant to you and can be cast away. This clearance
    strategy might mean a batch of emails, texts or phone
    calls to wrap up unfinished conversations or open-
    ended discussions.

Good luck with your milk pan strategy; you will be
astounded by how good it feels when you take a step forward
in this way. You may not tie up all those loose ends but the
purposeful way you raise your awareness and your action
will diminish many previously undetected energy drains.

35

PERSONAL BOARD OF DIRECTORS

> "In everyone's life, at some time, our inner fire goes out. It is then burst into flame by an encounter with another human being. We should all be thankful for those people who rekindle the inner spirit."
>
> Albert Schweitzer (1875–1965)

In my coaching work I have noticed how many senior executives and leaders carry complex decisions around with them and find themselves tackling these alone. You are never alone.

While working with a group of leaders and assisting their journeys to craft their unique way of leading, I returned to a reliable and extremely effective method of decision support.

That was to connect with the people who have influenced their path so far. Be they alive or dead, real or fictitious, advice and guidance can be garnered from these respected and admired influencers.

Grab a pen and paper, sit somewhere quiet for 10 minutes and think about the following:

- Who are the five people (more if you like) who have had an impact on your career and your decisions? People who you have admired, respected or perhaps even emulated or copied?

- Consider each of the names on your list. Pause and think about the person; think about the effect of influence they had on you, the circumstance, the outcome? Note down three words or short phrases that describe this. These people are the first non-executive directors of 'You PLC'.

- Next, bring to mind the biggest topic on your mind. This might be the decision that you have not yet reached, the issue you are still contemplating or the choice you have not yet made. Maybe even the subject that is interfering with your sleep or wellbeing.

Randomly choose two people from your list and 'ask' their view of your topic. What advice do they have?

Remember, you don't have to take the advice, just consider the different view. Does it move you forward, does it present more questions whatever the particular style or approach may be?

You get to choose your board of directors. You can even sack them! I have worked with clients who have added family members, admired fictional characters and characters from the public eye whom they understand and respect.

Enjoy your next board meeting, and keep it simple.

36

UPGRADE YOUR INNER CRITIC

> "Courage is what it takes to stand up and speak; courage is also what it takes to sit down and listen."
>
> Winston Churchill (1874–1965)

I relish the opportunity and challenge of public speaking, particularly at business conferences. At an event in 2010 my challenge was to create a lasting positive change to attitude and self-belief in 45 minutes. The audience were experiencing massive organisational change and an unstable market place. My topic was Personal Resilience.

I was very aware in the lead-up to this event, more so than before, of the power of my inner voice. The frightened, damning Inner Critic!

As I prepared my talk the voice spoke (loudly), full of doubt and posing unhelpful questions: Will I have any impact at all? Is the content right? Is there enough or too much?

The neutralising force in the prep stage was my wife. In her own special, grounded and pragmatic way she told me to stop worrying and get on with it: you'll be fine and the content is great.

On the day of the event I met other presenters and was aware of my Inner Critic comparing me to them, pouring on more doubt. Would I be credible? Who do I think I am? They are so much more professional than me…

Maybe you have an active Inner Critic too, which speaks from the scared ego, pulling you back to the safe low-risk, sometimes do-nothing place. It may accelerate nerves and anxiety, and make you feel full of doubt.

But this doesn't have to be the case. There are many coping methods I have used when coaching others on how to speak and present. A more permanent change for you is to upgrade your Critic instead of just quietening him or her.

1. First, get explicit about and evaluate your expectations for the talk. What are your hopes and intentions for

it? What could they be? This last question is difficult to answer if the Critic is already in conversation but, when asked earlier, it can raise your game.

2. Next, tune in to the inner voices. The Critic may be yattering, but so will the Encourager, albeit much more quietly. Every time the Critic makes a comment, notice how you feel. Physiologically, you slump. This is not good. And if you begin your presentation in this state you are more likely to stumble, stutter and fluff. When your Encourager makes a comment and you actually hear it, you may not necessarily instantly become full of joy, but you will be calmer.

Notice both your Critic and your Encourager.

When the Critic makes a comment, don't listen. Choose another thought (often the absolute opposite) and keep thinking about it (for extra help here read the Thought Management 101 Simple Note).

Don't forget that you get to choose who you listen to.

Like my experience with the Personal Resilience conference speech, within a few minutes of taking these two upgrade steps, the Critic actually upgrades and begins to help instead of hinder (and the presentation went extremely well, thank you for asking!).

Keep calm and carry on!

37

LIBERATION FROM 'OUGHT TO'

> ""You will become as small as your controlling desire; as great as your dominant aspiration."
>
> **James Allen (1864–1912)**

Your choices are vast, even though you may spend most of your time unaware of the available choices as you follow the same habitual choosing process, complaining that things just don't get better.

Your everyday reality is directly related to two things:

1. What we think about (persistently).

2. The direction of travel (i.e. the actions we repeatedly take).

I often notice the gripping power of a particular underlying thought which, when left untouched, saps your power and enjoyment as you unconsciously think more of the same.

This is the 'ought to'.

Wrapped up in the decision-making unit inside your mind is a 'want to', 'need to', 'should do', 'could do' and of course, the mystifying 'ought to'.

In order to feel better and enjoy a sense of progress, satisfaction, achievement and joy, these thoughts need distilling before they entangle and get treated as if they were all the same.

A simple distillation:

Want Tos – never get enough of your time, and are instead given a back seat. They contain enjoyment and access to more of your potential. Carve out time and give them more focus immediately, be assertive here.

Need Tos – are often essential parts of your everyday life. If you like them, go there. If you don't, outsource and/or automate them, but don't ignore them.

Should Dos – are need tos with less power. Decide whether they can be upgraded or just let them go; they take up space and energy and drain you quickly as they accumulate.

Could Dos – are interesting and often more creative future-orientated change steps. Create some quality time and let your mind expand your could dos. They can be the catalyst thoughts for your future and need to be allowed some quality airtime.

Ought Tos – This is the one that intrigues me most of all. These could be like any of the other four, but lie angrily dormant, niggling and causing you discomfort, until you take some action on them.

What are the ought tos on your mind? Spend more time with relatives, work out more, eat better, plan more, get organised, change a habit?

Ought tos are often poorly categorised wants, needs, shoulds or coulds. They need immediate and regular sorting for your own well-being and evolution.

Here's a simple and liberating step:

Begin a list and spend the next week adding your ought tos to the list as they come to mind.

Add four columns to the right of your list.

In the first, rate how important each could be to you out of five (where five is potentially life-changing for the better).

In the second column rate each out of five in terms of how truly inspired you are right now to take action (where five is this very moment!).

In the third column multiply the previous two numbers.

Identify and highlight the top three scores in your list. For each of these write a single action you could take today to move in the direction of your 'ought to' (add this in the fourth column).

Take that action – you will feel surprisingly good and will have begun a new momentum in the direction of your inner desires.

The sooner you embark on this the sooner your reality will change. Revisit this exercise every three months to dramatically and permanently transform your world.

38

....

SIMPLE MEDITATION

> "All of man's problems derive from our inability to sit quietly in a room and do nothing."
>
> Friedrich Nietszche (1844–1900)

In the coaching world, meditation is a much talked-about technique for relaxing the mind and accessing more of one's hidden potential. For years I resisted the concept of meditation as a practice requiring incense, a cross-legged posture and Tibetan bowls, about which I was sceptical and for which I was under-resourced.

What I have learnt, however, is the power of simply *stopping* for even the shortest period of time, and allowing busy thinking to subside.

Brain research suggests that your mind operates up to sixteen times faster than your body and your speech. So it is not surprising that we can sometimes get entangled in multiple-layer thinking, losing focus and, often, experiencing serious fatigue.

Simple meditation is just that – simple. It doesn't necessarily require all the associated items such as incense or soothing music, although they will of course enhance the experience when you find the types that assist you. It is about stopping conscious activity for as little as two minutes.

Here's a way to introduce simple meditation into your schedule this week:

Take a seat in as clear a location as possible, away from interruptions and peripheral noise.

Breathe in and out naturally, but slowly. Count out 10 sets of an inhale and an exhale. Then count back down to one.

Just concentrate on your breathing and nothing else, let the thoughts come and go (sometimes picturing the number of the breath in your mind's eye helps).

That's it!

The busier you are the more difficult this challenge will be, but the greater the impact you will experience. On occasions you will lose track of your counting as you follow a thought. Begin again from one.

To astound yourself with the benefits of this process, repeat at the same time each day for a week: get your mind and body used to the time and place and simply STOP!

39

RETURN ON INVESTMENT OF YOUR TIME

> "I expect to pass through this world but once. Any good therefore that I can do, or any kindness that I can show to any fellow creature, let me do it now. Let me not defer or neglect it, for I shall not pass this way again."
>
> William Penn (1644–1718)

Many of my clients have such packed schedules; they feel like they are being whipped along in a fast-flowing river, with little power to change direction. A frequent outcome is that some weeks they feel good (and inspired), others they feel bad (and drained) and all points in between. Are you leaving your outcome to fate, allowing the river and its course to have control?

Becoming more deliberate about where you invest your time can, in effect, become a tiller to steer your course along your river. Ask yourself:

- *Where do I spend my time?*
- *What is the impact on me during those investments?*

Take last week for example. Let's say, for argument's sake, you worked fifty hours. What is the typical split of your time across the following investment categories?

Self – time in your own space, unhindered, uninterrupted, focused or unfocused, reflecting or in action, just time with yourself.

Inspiring – with people or in places that inspire or motivate you, which cause you to think differently, garner new ideas or feed your reflective time.

The Norm – with people or in places that comprise your typical and everyday current 'norm' as you know it. Occasionally challenging, but where you are mostly in control of the situation with few surprises.

Drain – with people, places or tasks that simply take your energy levels right down.

It doesn't take Sherlock Holmes to make the link between your time investment and the feel-good or feel-bad outcome.

Do the analysis, become aware, then shift your schedule.

1. Minimise 'drain' time immediately.
2. Increase 'inspiring' time. This can take a little extra thought and effort as you seek out opportunities. Space will open up to do this in the next category.
3. Get some 'self time' – now! Schedule it, protect it, improve it week after week. This is your key to unlocking your potential.

40

DECIDING YOUR FUTURE

> "If you want to know your past – look into your present conditions. If you want to know your future – look into your present actions."
>
> **A Chinese proverb**

An inspirational chap named Mike Dooley writes extensively on one of my favourite topics: 'Thoughts become things'. In a typical example from one of his brief articles (www.tut. com), he writes:

'Resist the temptation to base today's decisions upon today's facts and circumstances, which are little more than what remains of yesterday's decisions. Instead, base them upon the facts and circumstances as they will inevitably be, once your dreams have already come true.'

So, base your thinking and decisions on where you want to be, not where you are (otherwise you are simply building a stay-here strategy).

I recently worked with a client to design the business that he deeply desired. He and I included a category of clients that he would be excited and eager to work with but, as yet, did not have. We talked about this new category, what it would be like working with these clients and how this would fit into his schedule and other activities – in essence, making decisions based on future circumstances.

Within two weeks he received an enquiry from someone exactly in this new category. It works!

By activating the possibility and beginning to think about the opportunity, we had set in place the Law of Attraction (you get what you think about). The unconscious and conscious decisions made by the client every day moved him closer to the new possibility, noticing people and events that matched his desire. The faster you do this and the clearer you are, the faster it happens.

It sounds so simple that most people simply don't take the first step. It even seems too simple to bother trying (which, by the way, is the reason why most people brilliantly recreate what they've already got, whether they like it or not).

Even if the future circumstances are nothing like today, still include them in your thinking.

41

SIMPLIFYING RESOLUTIONS

> "The starting point of all achievement is desire. Keep this constantly in mind. Weak desires bring weak results, just as a small amount of fire makes a small amount of heat."
>
> Napoleon Hill (1883–1970)

Although it is possible at any time of year, January is the greatest reason or nudge we have to make a change, cease a bad habit or take action on that subject we have always said we would.

According to the Opinion Corporation of Princeton, New Jersey:

- 62% of people make New Year's resolutions.
- 8% are always successful.
- 19% of people achieve resolutions every other year.
- 49% have infrequent success.
- 24% never succeed and have failed on every resolution every year.

That's 1 in 4 people who fail each and every time!

I have noticed that people have acquired a level of flippant cynicism and acceptable failure regarding our ability to resolve.

Here are a few thoughts to simplify and perhaps enable the change you truly desire – a chance to get through the fog of doubt.

Don't have any resolutions – if you are reading this, then you are clearly interested in your development and you are already on a path of resolution not linked to January.

Find the compulsion – what are the three compelling reasons why this resolution needs to happen? Write them down and remind yourself often (affix sticky notes on your PC screen, write on the tiles in your shower, anything to keep them in mind).

Spotlighting – create a totem/poster/image of your situation with resolution achieved. Keep this in view every day.

Choose one – lots of evidence now suggests that humans can only point willpower in one direction at a time.

Make a regular appointment – put a recurring 30-minute appointment in your diary every week to assess, review and revitalise your resolution.

Find a resolution buddy – and motivate them in exchange.

Follow the feeling – if it doesn't feel right in January or February, let it go. You may cause unnecessary pain by hanging on to what isn't right actually for you at this time.

Make it physical – is there some physical/visual change you can make to signify the restart? Maybe move your office around, clear out your wardrobe of clothes that no longer serve you or put your watch on the opposite wrist.

Automate it – simplify and ease the action or steps leading to the action, to the maximum extent that you can (e.g. if it is going to the gym more often, prepare several exercise kits and put them by the door or in the car).

Reward yourself – set reward thresholds and, crucially, deliver on the rewards you promise yourself when the thresholds are met (not before!); for example a weekend away or a new phone.

May your resolve gain strength, and achievement become your norm.

42

···

FOCUS ON ONE

> "The secret of getting ahead is getting started. The secret of getting started is breaking your complex overwhelming tasks into small manageable tasks, and then starting on the first one."
>
> Mark Twain (1835–1910)

I have noticed consistently with coaching clients that there is one action that, when committed to, produces certain new results. But more often than not they get lost in a list of perhaps overwhelming actions that eventually develop into resistance, boredom and lack of progress.

So what is the answer?

Well, you are probably bombarded with meetings, events, options, information and challenges, each grasping at your concentration and focus. Face it, it is tough work to make personal change stick.

My research concurs with that of many schools and institutions that have studied willpower. Like a laser, it is strongest when focused on *one* thing.

At the beginning of a particular year I carried three 'resolutions' and experienced the challenge of a triple willpower demand. I then made the decision to choose just one item and pointed all my willpower at the challenge. In making this choice, the challenge or resolution remained intact and was achieved within the month.

As month two began, I could then chose a new single focus, and in turn, nothing became more important than that.

I challenge you to audit your must-do, need-to and have-to lists and zoom in on one thing for this week or this month and do it.

You will strengthen your ability to focus on any one thing and be capable of more developmental and transformational change. You will develop a new powerful single-item achievement muscle.

So make it just one thing and you will succeed.

43

PUT YOUR FACE BACK WHILE IT'S STILL WARM

> "Experience is not what happens to you. Experience is what you DO with what happens to you."
>
> Aldous Huxley (1894–1963)

One of my favourite phrases from renowned author and speaker Wayne Dyer is: 'If you change the way you look at things, the things you look at change' – i.e. the attitude you have at any moment predetermines how you experience everything that's going on.

Your reality (how it feels to be you with all your pressures, joys, successes and tensions) obviously feels absolutely real.

And without giving it any conscious thought, it seems to simply be what it is – real, without any options. It just is.

The way you view your reality (your mindset) sets up your behaviour: what you cause and what you experience.

The truth is, your situation is probably quite different to what you're telling yourself. Which bits of it are you noticing and focusing on the most?

To change your reality (and you can) you need to be ready to defy it! Let me illustrate.

Over a three week period some time ago I found I was carrying an attitude of 'I've got loads to do and too little time', plus a bit of 'I don't know where to start', with a dash of 'I'm not actually getting anywhere' thrown in. This was a potent mix that left me feeling tense and at times anxious and irritable (e.g. reacting impatiently with loved ones). I wore this attitude in my facial expressions too, and in these situations my wife would often tell me to "put your face back while it's still warm", as my grimace remained in place for too long.

During this period she also had been carrying an unhelpful attitude, one of 'I never have time to focus'.

Put these together and the 'reality' in our home and work situation had become tense, frantic and rushed. We were achieving a lot, perhaps, but it didn't always feel like fun along the way.

You can always find a moment to view Facebook, turn on the TV or read something irrelevant, anything that disproves your mindset. So here's a suggestion which shifts attitudes and alters how we experience our days:

A reality check.

Explore a way to defy your current reality, to the extent that you just about still believe in it. You may not be able to convince yourself of the complete opposite mindset (such as 'I have abundant time to achieve everything today'), but you might be able to get closer to that ideal: 'I have time', 'I get things done', 'I find time'.

Find three proofs that the alternate reality is already true. Work hard at this detective work as your mind will initially resist.

When feelings and thoughts of the old mindset creep back in; consciously and deliberately shift your thinking to the reality you actually want (or one that feels better).

It will not take long to work this through and very soon your shifted reality will become the norm.

44

THE 3–4–3 STRATEGY

> "The road to happiness lies in two simple principles: find what it is that interests you and that you can do well, and when you find it put your whole soul into it – every bit of energy and ambition and natural ability you have."
>
> John D. Rockefeller III (1906–1978)

Apart from being what I consider to be the best football formation, 3–4–3 has become a successful way to shift my clients' behaviour towards spending more time doing and being what they are designed to do and be.

Whenever I meet a team, client or participants in a workshop, I often ask how much of their time could be described as being at their best. How effective did they consider themselves to be at that particular moment? Then out come the stories about the volume of work, meetings etc. that get in the way of operating at their peak. And some brilliant justifications for why most of their working days are spent this way.

The 3–4–3 strategy works like this.

Think about everything involved in doing your job. Everything!

Top Three – approximately 30% of what you do or get involved in is what makes you go 'ooh'. You are great at it; time seems to slip past when you're doing it; no one else could ever do it quite to your standards; when you've completed these things you actually feel better. It may take time, but it certainly doesn't seem to take effort. These are the things that, if you spent all your time doing them and not the other stuff, you would be an unstoppable machine!

Bottom Three – at the other end of the ratio are 30% of the things that you are poor at, you probably put them off until they build up and shout at you; when you are working on them, you feel drained and uninspired and your mind wanders. You begin to detest the task and everything and everyone associated with it; you look for and take any distraction from it; you're inefficient at these things and they take an achingly disproportionate length of time.

Middle Four – in the middle you've got the rest: 40% of the things you do are okay; part of the job, expected and known – you know they've got to be done and you get them done.

The juicy opportunity for you is to get to a point where you are aware of the top three and bottom three items.

Make an active decision to spend more time doing your top three – don't put them off, waiting until you've suffered and done the nasty things. Maybe consider a compromise and do one of the middle four for every one of the top three.

Next, make an active decision to spend less time on the bottom three. Don't kid yourself that everything will be fine when these are done, because it won't – it will be exactly the same or even worse because you have missed the opportunity of making dramatic positive change with your top three. Look to outsource these tasks: delegate them, ask a friend to help and get them done or even pay someone to do so because, and this is the magic bit – the items in your bottom three will be in someone else's top three!

And as for the middle four, you'll always get these done somehow. Hidden within them may even be your potential, a new currently unrefined skill. Observe others, explore new learning and utilise the time you are saving from your no longer draining bottom three.

Bonus Refined 3–4–3 Nugget:
The Art of Successful Delegating.

You know you need to delegate and haven't yet cracked how to make it work for yourself or the delegated helper. The 3–4–3 strategy is made for you.

It is highly likely that up until now, whenever you need to free up time, the tasks you delegate come from your top three or middle four, simply because you cannot believe anyone else would want to do your bottom three laundry.

And of course the delegatee can never complete those top three tasks to your standard and expectations or with the essence and spice that you would give, so you spend your time looking over their shoulder and end up taking the damn thing back!

But there in your bottom three are tasks that you feel nothing for, that someone else (if you choose them correctly) will do well, faster and with less pain, because it falls within their top or middle categories.

You get the gist, so become aware and make your move!

45

CONTROL–ALT–DELETE

> "We cannot change anything until we accept it."
>
> Carl Jung (1875–1961)

One of the first actions I take when my PC becomes irritatingly slow at processing tasks is press 'Control–Alt–Delete'. This rudimentary step displays the processes running and the amount of the computer's memory power working on each. The absence of further useful knowledge means that I rarely do anything with this information but am always curious about what the processes are – are they important, are they good for me, does my PC need to have them at all?

Coaching dialogues are the mind version of 'Control–Alt–Delete', uncovering the plethora of processes, thoughts, tasks and to-dos you are working on.

Just like my cluttered PC, your list can be incredibly long. Every item uses some of your power/focus/RAM. Every loose piece of paper on your desk, notes around the home, calls yet to be returned, active tasks, dormant tasks, old mistakes, new ideas, plans, dreams, doubts. All of these use up part of your processing power.

Your brilliant capacity means much of this goes unnoticed and you go about your day comfortably. As the list grows beyond normal and acceptable levels, however, your capacity to be at your best and energy to work on new things and challenges can become exhausted.

My challenge for you in this Simple Note is to press your personal Control–Alt–Delete. Grab a pen and paper and make the list. Stay with the list and go beyond the obvious.

For best results work on this with a colleague (or even a coach!) and possibly keep returning to your list over the course of a few days as new 'processes' come to mind.

Now review your list. There may be obvious items that necessarily use up the majority of your memory power, and that tends to be where we apply our focus.

Next, notice the long, long list of seemingly insignificant things that when combined take up space in your capacity and use up yet more energy. This list requires an immediate purge.

What can you complete, let go of and action right now?

Make these decisions and you WILL notice the difference.

Consider installing 'Control–Alt–Delete' as part of your personal maintenance programme, monthly or more frequently if the list seems long.

46

SOME LIGHT WEEDING

"Don't judge each day by the harvest you reap, but by the seeds you plant."

Robert Louis Stevenson (1850–1894)

I am blessed with a great garden, but would not describe myself as a gardener, or being in any way especially motivated to work on a flower bed. However, while walking around the garden in the sun one morning the weeding metaphor struck me once again.

Looking around I could see that the weeds, although not yet dominant, were many and thriving. Within a few weeks they would dominate the beds and prevent the desired plants from flourishing. It doesn't seem urgent right now to attend to the weeds but, once done, the space for growth expands, and even creates the opportunity to add new plants. In both cases this minimises the space for weeds to return.

You get the metaphor? Your mind, desk, plans, shelves, diaries all attract weeds. They seem unimportant and inoffensive until you reach the point where concentration suffers, focus is hindered, you tire quickly and lose sight of your goal. Progress has slowed without you noticing and the dream gets lost.

Even if it is not yet spring, it is always a good time to weed out the unwanted, create some space and allow the good stuff to grow, and the new ideas and initiatives to be planted.

My challenge to you is to schedule 30 minutes this week to:

1. Weed your desk, your diary, your involvement in peripheral projects. Spot them, decide on them, delete them and remove them.
2. Become mindful of and reduce your watching, reading or listening to negative news, negative people.
3. Fill any obvious gaps with meeting positive and inspiring people, places or events.

47

....

WHAT ARE YOU READING?

"Be careful the environment you choose for it will shape you; be careful the friends you choose for you will become like them."

W. Clement Stone (1902–2002)

It's just a question, but one worthy of an answer. During a normal week your attitude, mental state, mood and state of being are influenced by the many external stimuli to which you are exposed (deliberately or not).

Simply to accept what is coming at you and to consume what is in front of you is a dangerous strategy. To be generally unaware of what is coming at you is also a dangerous strategy.

This Simple Note focuses specifically on what you read, and it equally applies to what you watch on TV, listen to on the radio, the conversations you have, the places you visit and so on.

I gave up reading a daily paper many years ago, as I began to notice that some of the content changed my mood, affecting the ensuing minutes, hours or sometimes the whole day.

Yes, there will be stuff you need to read and absorb in order to help you in your job, your career, to follow your passion and your interests. But everything else should go. It will not disappear on its own. In fact, the volume of unsolicited unhelpful, disempowering messages from multiple sources is increasing.

Observe yourself over the next week. After reading the newspaper, run an internal audit of your mood: what articles remain in your thoughts and how do you feel about them?

If it doesn't feel good, give it up NOW.

You are at your best when you feel good so stop spoiling the good stuff and reduce the inputs that take you off track.

48

THE MOST IMPORTANT MEETING

"You are today where your thoughts have brought you; you will be tomorrow where your thoughts take you."

James Allen (1864–1912)

A quick view of your calendar for the upcoming week will undoubtedly reveal days full of meetings, back-to-back on some occasions, with no breathing space between.

The culture of many companies in which I have been involved seems to dictate the meeting habit. Meetings are invaluable, most of the time, in achieving an objective or two. However I have observed their ability to consume teams, divisions and even entire companies. Far too many people are involved in them and the agendas and action lists lengthen. Both are recipes for reduced effectiveness.

But one particular type of meeting, potentially the most valuable to you and your journey, almost always gets pushed out or even forgotten.

My challenge in this Simple Note is that you immediately schedule this **most important meeting**. It is simply a meeting with yourself. The 'you-on-you' meeting can be strategic or tactical, and have similar intent to the plethora of meetings you would otherwise attend each day.

You may convince yourself that you already have meetings with yourself as you snatch a moment to contemplate a project, an intention or an initiative. But until they are formally included in your schedule they are almost always sub-optimal! They only occur as you walk between other meetings, to the car park or the train, on the journey itself, fitted into the gaps with no agenda or focus. They are random thoughts that are open to every possible distraction, and almost always in utterly inappropriate environments.

Would you seriously allow your team or project meetings to take place like that? If you did, what result would you expect from them?

If you want to shift your thinking, performance and results, then you need a 'you-on-you' communication plan. Your meeting need not necessarily be in a conference room with PowerPoint slides, just set it up in a way that you will be at your best. Hold it in a quiet place, for as long as you can handle being the single participant. And don't complicate it, just have one or two agenda items/thoughts to focus on (and you won't be surprised to know that I recommend just one).

Ten minutes a day? An hour a week? You could even invite expert guests (your coach, mentor or development buddy) to join you. Create some frequency; perhaps even make notes (Einstein did). Just stop putting off this incredibly valuable investment of your time.

Just do it.

49

YOU'RE HERE NOW, NOWHERE ELSE – ACT LIKE IT

> "Our self image and our habits tend to go together. Change one and you will automatically change the other."
>
> Dr. Maxwell Maltz (1899–1975)

One of my coaches, Drew Rozell, provided much inspiration to me during our work together and in the articles that he penned. He asserted the title phrase a few years ago in one of his newsletters – I still carry it with me and recite it often.

Have you been in situations or places where you would rather be somewhere else? Were some of your thoughts and attention elsewhere anyway? Have you been at an event, meeting or situation that simply wasn't pushing your buttons, but it was not appropriate for you just to walk away?

In such situations, you have become a person of two minds: less than fully effective, your concentration is impaired, your creativity is hindered, your mood shifts (in the wrong direction), you're probably less fun to be with and it is simply not a good place to be.

Over the next few days try to notice 'you are here now, nowhere else, act like it', in all circumstances in which you find yourself. Does your mind wander? Do you feel fidgety or irritable?

Here are five thought-starters to shift you quickly to the more powerful single-minded place:

1. If I absolutely loved this situation what would I be doing or saying, how would I be standing, talking, contributing? Whatever your answer, do it.
2. What have I not yet noticed about this situation – people, objects, sounds, attitudes, moods?
3. What might be my role here, assuming I haven't realised it fully yet?
4. If there is something for me to learn here, what might it be?
5. If there is something for me to teach or share here, what might it be?

Carry these questions or some of your own design into the next week's meetings. A soon as you catch yourself drifting off the beat, pose a question, answer and act on your responses.

Enjoy, be fully present and thrive with your single mind.

50

THE FIVE PEOPLE WHO INFLUENCE YOU MOST

"If you always live with those who are lame, you will yourself learn to limp."

Latin proverb

The five people with whom you spend most time have the greatest impact on:

1. Your mood.
2. Your attitude.
3. Your thinking and view of the world.
4. Your range of default decisions.
5. Your vision and hope for the future.

Consciously or unconsciously this select group of people are shaping your thinking, sharing their ideas and views and providing the space for you to share yours.

If there is something about your mood or attitude or current circumstance that isn't quite right, or is in some way off track, then look again at your high-influence five. Are they actually serving you, your goals, your desires? Do they stretch, support, challenge? Are they even bothered about your personal growth?

Once you have identified the five, consider what is going on in their world. What is their focus and are they on the up or down?

This group is often in place as a result of recent history or your geographical location. Until this group is configured by conscious design, your ability to shift your mood, attitude and results will be difficult.

Of your current panel, whom do you need to reduce your exposure to? Who could join? Who will support you and gear you up for greater things?

Take action this week. The change action you need to take may be major; in which case start now. You could even begin 'interviewing' potential candidates to join your team.

51

THE PURPOSEFUL TEAM

> "Pleasure in the job puts perfection in the work."
>
> Aristotle (384 BC–322 BC)

Many of the teams with whom I have been involved, as a member or as a coach and facilitator, find themselves just existing, simply delivering the stream of actions that are required and occasionally a few more.

Within you and your team is a nagging sense that more is possible. I am sure you have often heard the 1+1=3 synergy story, the sum of the parts, etc. And indeed significant greater potential lies just in reach for your team.

Consider this simple line of enquiry for your team, and allow the answers to guide your way ahead.

1. *What do I personally want or get from being part of a team?*

    Responses from the group will be different; bringing them to the surface helps each team member realise that we all can achieve our own desires, together.

2. *Who are our customers?*

    These include stakeholders, contributors, actual customers who buy your products and services, suppliers and everyone on whom your team has impact.

3. *What do they say about us?*

    You could even ask them, although they may already be communicating in verbal and non-verbal ways.

4. *What do we want them to say about us?*

    Be as adventurous and as outrageous as you can, stretch beyond what seems possible from where you are.

5. *What stops you?*

    Design the Change. This means clearing out the barriers to progress. Start with the easy changes and build belief and momentum from there.

This is the unconscious strategy for all successful teams. Making it conscious will begin the change journey for yours.

52

JUDGING YOURSELF

> "Trust yourself. You know more than you think you do."
>
> Benjamin Spock (1903–1998)

While in conversation with a coaching client, I noticed how often she was judging herself and the situations in which she found herself. Unconsciously judging whether they were good enough or whether she was good enough, comparing herself against some unconscious, unspecified, impossible-to-attain criteria. The speed with which the judgments kicked in instantly affected her attitude and mood, the words and tone of voice and the amount of joy she was allowing herself to experience. When the judge runs out of control absolutely nothing seems good enough.

Have you got a judge that jumps in quickly and causes the same? This judge is not helpful. For most of us it is holding some ridiculous perfect world situations or versions of yourself that are delusional and make it easy to beat yourself up or set yourself up for disappointment.

Stop judging. It hurts, it doesn't feel good in the moment it judges or in any of those that follow.

I challenge you to go one week without judging anything.

An alternate course of action is to notice your judge pontificating – perhaps make a note of the judgement in a book, laugh at it, then leave it alone. Accept yourself and the situations that show up as if they were great, even if they don't appear to be.

One week with no judging is good – relish it, it's okay. These situations don't have to be anything else; they don't need to be better or worse, faster or slower, just whatever they are.

Go on, try it for just one week. It will kick the judge out.

During your week there is a chance you will experience:

- The judge screaming at you to be heard (pull the metaphorical wig over her or his face).
- People noticing you acting differently and asking if you're okay!

- Things feeling 'lighter' and not as disastrous as those around you may suggest.
- Your ego panicking that you are missing something (not true).
- An amazing feeling of 'everything is okay'!

Good luck and keep it simple.

And your end of year bonus…

53

THINKER THINKS, PROVER PROVES

> "What we think, we become."
>
> Buddha

Any hypothesis or assumption you are holding tends to be how you set yourself up to experience the day, what you see, hear, feel and notice.

You may often not even be aware what your active assumptions are, since they have been formed over the years without you realising and become ingrained quite deeply, as a product of:

1. Your parenting.
2. Your friends.

3. What you read and watch and consume.
4. Who you spend most of your time with.

Your assumptions are at work and in place in all areas of your life and they dictate the ease, the success and the joy you derive from:

1. Relationships.
2. Work, your job role and the success you achieve.
3. Health and wellbeing.
4. Finances.

At some level of consciousness you are constantly thinking and embedding these assumptions. The rest of your brain is at work scouring your world to prove them to be true. Your sensory tool kit is off finding evidence to confirm the hypothesis. The Thinker thinks, the Prover proves.

Where you find exceptions, whether you welcome or detest them, you relate to them as rare and incorrectly aligned happenings and in effect reject them.

As an example, a long-time client of mine was continuing to experience career success, but always coupled with work overload, physical demands and time pressures that affected her entire life. In dialogue we discovered that deep in the background was her assumption that she would always struggle in senior roles and with greater responsibility came greater struggle. While not deluding her that senior roles do not bring new and stretching challenges, the extent to which it was affecting her did not necessarily have to be true. Unknowingly, she was proving to herself that her assumption was true.

So we experimented with new hypotheses, ones that her mind might just be able to accept may be true: In senior roles, opportunities frequently present themselves to change ways of working. A peaceful existence may be possible! And slowly, these new hypotheses began to get proven too. Resistance and doubt surfaced (thank goodness for subsequent coaching conversations) but the assumption at work was challenged and changed.

My challenge to you now is to consider what assumptions you hold in the four areas (relationship, work, health and financial success). Then take a look at your current and recurring results: they will be an almost direct match to the assumptions you make.

Could you upgrade one of them?

Your brilliant brain can go about proving whatever you task it to do. Choose something nice!

FINDING YOUR OWN SIMPLE WAY

Congratulations, you've reached the end of this collection of Simple Notes. Taken one a week, you may have explored a year's worth of personal evolution ideas, or perhaps have dipped in specifically to the Simple Notes that match your current growth focus. I hope that you have found a number of Simple Notes to support your journey, shift your thinking and challenge you to change. Stephen Covey states very specifically in his work (most notably *The Seven Habits of Highly Effective People*) that to really embed new information, go and teach it to someone else within a few days. This paradigm shift (from learner to teacher) helps the brain connect with the information in different ways; often helping us to 'get it' even more deeply than when you were simply a learner.

So why not go and teach this stuff? All I ask is that you mention this book and my work and if it helps another then they can find their way to me and the store of even more Simple Notes. Teach them, discuss them, work on them alone, with a partner or as a team. A number of people have told me that when they have worked through one or more of the Simple Notes, new ideas emerge and the ensuing solution is even better.

Good luck, and keep it simple!

SOURCES OF INSPIRATION

Kate Duffy

I have known Kate since we were participants on a coaching programme ('Simply Effective' with Jay Perry and Scott Wintrip) in 2001. Since then we have coached each other, worked on client coaching projects and, together with Joanne Dunleavy, delivered the 'Attitude Vitamin' – a series of 15-minute inspirational ideas to shift your attitude – till 2009.

Kate Duffy is a Certified Life Coach with a natural results orientation. Currently her focus is in recruitment, 'People Finding', with her team at KDA. Kate's background includes Non Profit Leadership, Sales, Management Coaching and HR Business Partner. www.kateduffy.com.

Michael Neill

I have been reading Michael's work since 2002 as a subscriber to his blog and cannot recall a single one of his articles that has not been valuable to me. Michael Neill is an internationally-renowned success coach and the best-selling author of *You Can Have What You Want, Feel Happy Now!*, the *Effortless Success* audio program and *Supercoach: 10 Secrets to Transform Anyone's Life*. He has spent the past 20 years as a coach, adviser, friend, mentor and creative spark plug to celebrities, CEOs, royalty and people who want to get more out of their lives. His books have been translated into 10 languages, and his public talks and seminars have been well received at the United Nations and around the world.

Seán Weafer

Seán and I were thrust together to work on a coaching project with Ulster Bank and it wasn't long before our contrasting styles began to connect incredibly; the more we understood each other, the faster results took place. He is irrepressible and constantly in motion. He is an international speaker, author, trainer, coach and contract 'deal closer' on finding, closing and keeping B2B high-net-worth clients.

Drew Rozell

I have been an avid reader of the 'Drewsletter' since 2003, and Drew has always influenced my thinking. In 2009 I engaged him as my coach and worked with him for a year, one in which I acquired a new business and took significant change steps in the direction of my own coaching business. Drew holds a PhD in Social Psychology, and is a writer and personal coach who works with clients to raise their level of awareness and live more attractive lives. His work is now focused on living a very cool life, with a book and development programme to boot. www.verycoollife.com.

Thomas Leonard

To me he was a founding father of modern coaching, a prolific creator of content and a remarkable coach with whom I had the honour of working in two live events in London before his death in 2003. He founded Coach University in 1992, the International Coaching Federation in 1994, authored literally hundreds of coaching development classes and programmes and launched Coachville in 2000, which became my main source of learning and development. www.coachville.com www.thomasleonard.com.

Wayne Dyer

Wayne is perhaps my most absolute source of inspiration. His work is normally the first place I turn to for thoughts, ideas and what to do next. He has authored more than 30 books and created many audio programmes and videos that have changed my thinking and helped spawn ideas of my own. His books include *Manifest Your Destiny*, *Wisdom of the Ages*, *There's a Spiritual Solution to Every Problem* and the *New York Times* bestsellers *10 Secrets for Success and Inner Peace*, *The Power of Intention*, *Change Your Thoughts— Change Your Life*, and now *Excuses Begone!* have all been featured as National Public Television specials in the USA. He holds a Doctorate in Educational Counseling from Wayne State University and was an associate professor at St. John's University in New York.

....

SIMON TYLER AND
THE SIMPLE WAY

Simon has enabled scores of business executives, leaders, owners and solopreneurs to become increasingly successful by exploring their own intellect and applying a range of innovative and personally enabling techniques.

He is much respected for his ability to deliver refreshingly honest, acutely insightful and practical coaching programmes that challenge consensus thinking, break through barriers and redefine connections through the power of attitude.

He is an astute and perceptive coach who can rapidly transform cold coaching knowledge into powerful coaching capability, turning hollow coaching theory into a uniquely usable personal toolkit.

Simon is available to coach individuals and teams and to speak at team meetings, seminars and conferences. His talks are guaranteed to inspire, motivate and, most importantly, deliver results. Using humour and audience interaction, real-life stories and actual situations, yet sometimes raising crucially important personal topics, his style is light, lively, memorable and entertaining, but also pragmatic – full of easy to apply techniques and tools for each member of his audience to put to immediate use for themselves and their teams.

Simple Notes like the ones contained in this book are published by Simon every two weeks to subscribers. To join the free mailing list and begin receiving the notes visit www.simontyler.com and register.

The Simple Notes have grown out of Simon's belief that the simple way is the best way. You can watch Simon talking about The Simple Way and describing ways to simplify your thinking and shift your attitude and results at www.thesimpleway.tv.

Simon is married with three children and lives on a farm in Wiltshire in the west of England.

He can be contacted via his website www.simontyler.com